BLACK
ABOLITIONISTS
AND FREEDOM FIGHTERS

BLACK
ABOLITIONISTS
AND FREEDOM FIGHTERS

Kimberly Hayes Taylor

The Oliver Press, Inc.
Minneapolis

The Oliver Press, Inc.
Charlotte Square
5707 West 36th Street
Minneapolis, MN 55416-2510

Library of Congress Cataloging-in-Publication Data

Taylor, Kimberly Hayes, 1962-
  Black abolitionists and freedom fighters / Kimberly Hayes Taylor.
    p.   cm. — (Profiles)
  Includes bibliographical references and index.
  Summary: Profiles the lives of eight Afro-American leaders,
including Frederick Douglass, Harriet Tubman, and Booker T.
Washington, who were instrumental in abolishing slavery or helping
former slaves achieve full citizenship.
  ISBN 1-881508-30-7 (lib. bdg.)
  1. Afro-American abolitionists—Biography—Juvenile literature. 2.
Afro-Americans—History—19th century—Juvenile literature. [1.
Afro-Americans—Biography. 2. Afro-Americans—History—19th
century] I. Title. II. Series: Profiles (Minneapolis, Minn.)
E449.T244   1996
973'.0496073—dc20
                                          95-40260
                                            CIP
                                            AC

ISBN: 1-881508-30-7
Profiles XX
Printed in the United States of America

02 01 00 99 98 97 96   7 6 5 4 3 2 1

Contents

Not long *after the Emancipation Proclamation was
announced, this engraving appeared in* Harper's
Weekly *magazine. To the left of the newly freed
family are images depicting the evils of slavery; on the
right, blacks enjoy the fruits of their emancipation.*

Introduction

On January 1, 1863, United States president Abraham Lincoln issued the Emancipation Proclamation. This act abolished slavery in the Confederate states of the South that were at war with the federal government's Union army. Although Lincoln did not free the slaves living in the southern states that had remained loyal to the Union—Delaware, Maryland, Kentucky, and Missouri—black people throughout the country rejoiced when they heard the words of the proclamation: they would be "forever free." Two years later, the Thirteenth Amendment to the U.S. Constitution would finally end slavery throughout the entire United States.

By the time many of the black abolitionists and freedom fighters in this book were born, the institution of slavery in the United States already had a long history. The first Africans were brought to the American colonies

Sold by Dutch traders as indentured servants who would work for a number of years to earn their freedom, 20 Africans arrived in Jamestown, Virginia, in 1619.

as servants in 1619, but, by the 1640s, most of the African residents of North America were slaves. They had no rights of citizenship and almost no hope of ever gaining their freedom. When the American colonies revolted against the British government and became the United States of America in 1776, there were about 500,000 slaves—one-fifth of the population—in the newly "free" country. Before 1808, when the U.S. Congress prohibited the importation of slaves, an estimated 400,000 Africans had been brought to the United States.

Unlike other immigrants, who had come to the New World of their own accord, the Africans had little opportunity to better themselves. Instead, they were stripped of their names and denied their cultural heritage. Their owners were careful to keep them separated from other slaves who were from the same tribe and spoke the same native language. Slaves were often prohibited from gathering together, practicing a religion, or becoming literate. They could also be sold away at any time.

Slaves were not only denied the opportunities that other immigrants had, but they were also often subjected to brutal treatment by their masters. Slaveowners were free to discipline their slaves as they chose, and they could

This scene of a slave market in Africa shows a black man being restrained and inspected by whites who traded goods for Africans and then sold them as slaves in the Caribbean and North America.

beat and torture them. There were no laws to protect slaves against abuse or neglect or rape, and slaves had no rights to defend themselves or each other.

Soon after the United States had gained its independence from Britain, the northern states—beginning with Pennsylvania in 1780—were inspired by the revolutionary ideals of freedom to pass laws for the *emancipation*, or freeing, of slaves living in the North. In the southern states, however, slavery was highly profitable, and the South's agricultural economy depended upon slave labor to plant and harvest tobacco, sugar cane, rice, and cotton crops. Even southerners who owned no slaves defended the institution.

In 1793, Eli Whitney's invention of the cotton gin had made cotton much easier to process. Because its seeds and hulls could now be removed by machine rather than by hand, the amount of cotton that each slave could harvest increased dramatically. Cotton now brought in so much wealth that the South was not willing to give up its slave labor without a fight.

By 1860, there were 4 million slaves living in the South. Many Americans, especially those belonging to religious groups such as the Quakers and the Methodists, actively opposed slavery. During the 1800s, slavery was debated many times as the U.S. Congress proceeded to admit new territories into the Union as either free or slave states. The work of black antislavery activists and abolitionist groups such as the largely white American Anti-Slavery Society, as well as increasing violence between proslavery and antislavery forces in the territories

After the invention of the cotton gin, the Deep South turned to cotton as its major crop, and landowners felt they could not survive without slave labor.

of Kansas and Missouri, brought the issue to a crisis point. Finally, in 1861, following the 1860 election of President Abraham Lincoln, who opposed slavery, the nation erupted in a civil war.

Beginning at the time of the American Revolution, the black abolitionists and freedom fighters featured in this book strived to improve the lives of black people and to end slavery in the United States. While speaking out and writing against slavery, working with other blacks to create organizations, or helping slaves to escape, these

11

Dred Scott became famous when his 1857 fight for freedom from his master reached the U.S. Supreme Court. The Supreme Court justices (most of whom were from the South) denied Scott his freedom and stated that any attempt by Congress to curb slavery in new territories was unconstitutional.

men and women were influenced to act by their own experiences and beliefs and by the oppression they saw among the people around them.

Religion was important in the lives of many of these leaders. Richard Allen's faith led him to found one of the first black churches and to become the first African Methodist Episcopal bishop in the United States. Whereas Allen was able to establish religious institutions for blacks, Nat Turner's visions led him to attempt to bring about a Judgment Day for white slaveholders.

Sojourner Truth and Harriet Tubman were also deeply religious, and both believed that God hated slavery. While Truth was promoting abolition and women's rights before large audiences, Tubman was gaining fame as the "Moses" of her people, guiding hundreds of slaves to freedom on the Underground Railroad.

Like Sojourner Truth, Frederick Douglass and Henry Highland Garnet battled slavery from the podium. These two leaders, who escaped from slavery fairly early in their lives, had very similar careers, becoming renowned lecturers and writers and later serving as U.S. diplomats to black nations. Garnet advocated violent resistance against slavery, while Douglass was reluctant to promote rebellion. Although he came to believe that violence might ultimately prove necessary, Douglass saw the U.S. Constitution as black Americans' best hope for ending slavery and racial discrimination.

Booker T. Washington was committed to the belief that people can achieve economic self-sufficiency by working hard and learning skills. Once blacks were financially stable, he contended, they could then seek full equality with whites. Mary Church Terrell promoted the self-sufficiency that Washington preached as well as anti-discrimination legislation. She believed in black women forming strong communities and organizations to help each other gain economic independence and led picket lines against segregated businesses well into her eighties.

From Richard Allen, who participated in the American Revolution, to Mary Church Terrell, who lived to see the civil rights movement of the twentieth century, these black abolitionists and freedom fighters fought bravely to end slavery and secure equal rights for all African Americans in the United States.

Richard Allen (1760-1831) overcame racial discrimination among white Methodists and became the first bishop of the African Methodist Episcopal (AME) Church that he had helped to found.

1

Richard Allen
Leading in Spirit

*L*ong before the black members of St. George's Methodist Church walked out in protest, Richard Allen had been working to create a separate church for black Methodists in the Philadelphia, Pennsylvania, area. For his efforts, Allen experienced resistance from the black community outside the church—the "most respectable people of color in the city"—as well as from St. George's white elder, or congregational leader. Despite the opposition that he faced, Richard Allen would become the founder of one of the first African American churches in the United States.

On February 14, 1760, Richard Allen was born in Philadelphia to slaves who were owned by a Quaker lawyer named Benjamin Chew, who later became chief justice of Pennsylvania. While he was still a young child, Richard and his family were purchased by Stokely Sturgis. Following the sale, the Allen family was taken to the Sturgis property near Dover, Delaware.

While Richard was growing up in Delaware, changes were brewing in his home state. In 1780, when he was 20, the Pennsylvania legislature passed the new nation's first law that granted gradual emancipation. (Rhode Island and Vermont had abolished slavery outright earlier before they were states.) Under Pennsylvania's law, blacks born to slaves after 1780 would be freed, but not until they were 28 years old. So even in that "free" state, Richard would have remained a slave.

In 1777, the young Allen had "found religion." Responding to "the call" to become a preacher, he traveled from house to house, telling people about Jesus. Soon afterward, he joined a Methodist study group. At the time, many black people were becoming members of the Methodist Church, the Protestant denomination that John Wesley had founded in 1738. Along with its lively preaching and down-to-earth gospel message, blacks welcomed the church's antislavery stance. Although some white people refused to let their slaves join a church because they believed religion promoted discontent and laziness among the slaves, Sturgis allowed Allen and his older brother to attend church services twice a month after they had found religion.

John Wesley (1703-1791), the British founder of Methodism, believed that anyone—including poor blacks—could achieve salvation simply through faith in Jesus. Richard Allen wholeheartedly embraced this belief.

Soon Stokely Sturgis himself joined the Methodist Church. Early in 1780, after listening to a sermon about the evils of owning slaves, Sturgis agreed that Allen could earn his freedom. After six years of working for other whites, Allen was able to pay Sturgis the agreed-upon sum of $2,000. Finally, he was a free man.

During those years, while laboring at tasks that ranged from driving a delivery wagon during the American Revolution to cutting wood and making bricks, Allen preached the gospel to anyone who would listen. After the British surrendered in late 1781, Allen continued to preach, traveling across Delaware, Maryland, New York and Pennsylvania. On his journeys, he went either by himself or accompanied by white clergymen, and he spoke to both white and black assemblies. Allen was formally licensed as a Methodist minister in 1782.

In 1785, Methodist bishop Francis Asbury invited Allen to travel the Methodist Church circuit with him as far south as the Carolinas. Although it was considered an honor to be asked to go along, Allen refused the bishop's invitation because of the restrictions he had imposed on him. In the South, Allen would be preaching to slaves, but he would not be allowed to mingle with them. And although he would be provided with food and clothing, Allen's only income would come from whatever donations he might collect. He would also have to sleep

Francis Asbury (1745-1816) came to America from England as a missionary in 1771. While a bishop of the Methodist Church in North America, he would become a friend and a supporter of Richard Allen.

outside in the bishop's carriage while the bishop slumbered in a comfortable bed indoors.

Instead, Allen decided to travel Pennsylvania's "Lancaster circuit." Soon afterwards, the white elder of St. George's Methodist Church in Philadelphia asked him to speak to the congregation's black members. Allen arrived in Philadelphia in February 1786, thinking he would remain there for only a few weeks. But when his popularity caused the church's black membership to grow from only a handful to 42 individuals, Allen decided to remain at St. George's a while longer.

In the 1780s, Philadelphia's black population was growing rapidly because former slaves and free blacks were resettling there. Most of these new residents were uneducated and did not attend church regularly. Allen wanted to reach these people and wrote that he "saw a large field open in seeking and instructing my African brethren, who had been a long forgotten people."

Allen, now a free man, began preaching to the blacks of Philadelphia whenever and wherever he could, sometimes as often as five times a day. He established prayer meetings and, in 1786, helped to form a new organization that would provide blacks with both spiritual guidance and mutual assistance such as education and health care. The following year, Allen and Absalom Jones, another prominent black member of St. George's, wrote the preamble for the Free African Society. It stated that the organization was being formed "without regard to [any particular] religious tenets" in order to cure the "irreligious and uncivilized state" of blacks.

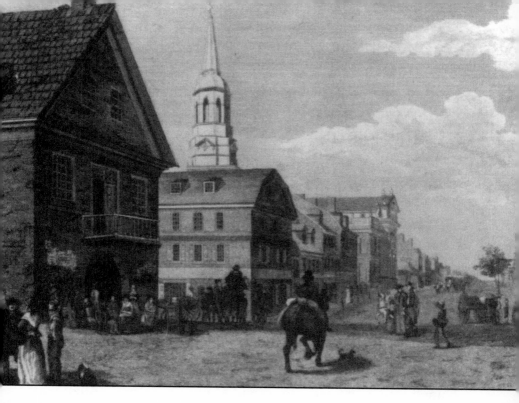

As the largest city in the free state of Pennsylvania, Philadelphia (shown in this 1799 engraving) became a haven for free blacks such as Richard Allen as well as escaped slaves from neighboring slave states.

At first, only Jones, Doras Giddings, and William White agreed with Allen that the Free African Society should have its own place of worship. The city's most prominent blacks opposed the idea of a separate black church, and the white elder at St. George's used "very degrading and insulting language" in informing Allen that he, too, did not approve of the idea.

Two years later, in 1788, Allen shocked many society members when he quit the group that he had helped to organize. Some believed he left because of his strong

Methodist faith. The Free African Society was a nondenominational group, with no specific religious ties. After Allen left the society, it continued to move toward becoming an independent black church. Wedding ceremonies were performed there, and regular Sunday morning worship services were first held in 1791.

During the following year (some accounts say 1793), the black walkout occurred at St. George's. Although none of the church's black members were slaves, they had no defense against discrimination since, at that time, blacks were not U.S. citizens. When St. George's white members decided they wanted a segregated church—one in which blacks and whites attended the same functions but sat apart from each other—it was clear that black people were also not thought of as equals in the church.

The congregation's black members were told they had to sit apart from the white members in the recently built balcony at the rear of the church instead of in the church's main pews. This new ruling seemed wrong to Allen and his fellow black Methodists. After all, they had "subscribed largely" (or donated money) for the church's remodeling project. Still, they honored the wishes of the white members and moved to the balcony. Later in the service, while the black worshippers were kneeling in prayer, one of the congregation's white officers tried to pull Absalom Jones to his feet and force him to the rear of the balcony. Jones asked to remain kneeling until the prayer was over, but he was told to move immediately.

At the conclusion of the prayer, all of the black people at the service got up and left the building. "We all went out of the church in a body," Richard Allen later wrote in his memoirs. "They were no more plagued with us in the church."

This incident clearly revealed to St. George's black membership their need for a separate place of worship. Although it had remained nondenominational, the Free African Society began raising funds for a new church building. A few society members opposed the plan, but most of them permitted their resources to be transferred into a church construction fund.

Because of their shared goal of building a house of worship, Allen decided once again to join the Free African Society. Along with Absalom Jones and William White, his former colleagues, and William Witcherly, Allen formed a committee that was responsible for fundraising and for securing a building site.

Although Allen's committee received the support of many local whites as well as the few remaining black members of St. George's, the elder who had earlier rejected the idea of a separate black church now threatened to expel from the Methodist Church all blacks who supported the new church. Allen and his fellow committee members argued that they had done nothing to justify their removal. Instead, they maintained that because they had been so "scandalously treated in the presence of all the congregation" at St. George's, they needed to have a place where they could worship freely.

When the committee had finally amassed enough money, they purchased property at Lombard and Sixth Streets. After Allen and the owner had agreed on a selling price, the other committee members instead decided to buy another piece of land on Fifth Street. Rather than forfeit the agreement, Allen kept the original lot.

Because building the church had been his idea, in 1793 Richard Allen "put the first spade in the ground" to officially begin its construction. While work on the first black church to be built in the United States proceeded, the parishioners had to decide whether or not they would remain a part of the Methodist Church. Both Allen and Jones favored retaining their Methodist ties, but the city's chief elder (the same elder who served at St. George's) "would neither preach for . . . nor have anything to do with" any blacks who wanted to have their own church. Although Allen was licensed to preach, he was not ordained as an elder or a deacon in the Methodist Church, so he could not officially perform any of the church's religious ceremonies such as baptism or marriage.

Feeling spurned by the Methodists, most of the group's leaders decided to join the Episcopal Church. They united with the Protestant Episcopal Church of America on August 12, 1794. When the new church's members asked Allen to serve as their minister, he refused because of his long-standing loyalty to the Methodist Church. Instead, Absalom Jones, who, like Allen, had voted for affiliating with the Methodists, accepted their offer and would become the United States's first black Episcopal priest. In 1796, his congregation was legally chartered as St. Thomas Episcopal Church.

Several months earlier, Allen and his supporters had met to discuss building a black Methodist church in

Philadelphia. They decided instead to buy an existing building, move it to Allen's property on Lombard and Sixth, and then remodel it to make a place for worship. Bishop Asbury, who had supported Allen's efforts, dedicated Bethel African Church in July 1794. Nearly five years later, on April 9, 1799, Asbury returned to ordain Richard Allen as a full-fledged Methodist deacon.

Allen's Bethel African congregation grew rapidly. By June 1803, its membership had reached 457. Two years later, a larger brick building was constructed to replace the original wooden structure.

Although Richard Allen had finally achieved his goal of a separate place of worship for Philadelphia's African Methodists, his congregation was still controlled by the white leaders at St. George's, the city's founding Methodist church. Because they did not understand the legal consequences, the Bethel African congregation had even been deceived when a white church official, who was following the prevailing policy, incorporated Bethel into the Methodist conference. This procedure took the property away from Allen and gave legal ownership to the Methodist Church.

Meanwhile, other black Methodist congregations were forming throughout the United States, and their members were experiencing the same difficulties as those at Bethel. This led Allen to organize a convention of black Methodist ministers to establish an independent denomination for African Methodists. On April 11, 1816, Allen became the group's first bishop and helped to write the bylaws that would govern the new African Methodist

Episcopal (AME) Church. Unlike the white Methodist Church, the AME Church dropped the position of elder and did not allow slaveowners to become members.

The actions of the black Methodists had mirrored those of other black religious groups in the United States at the turn of the nineteenth century. At a time when black people throughout the country were struggling to gain their freedom in society, black members of every Protestant denomination from Baptist to Episcopalian were establishing their own churches and battling their denominational leaders for the rights and benefits that white church members already had. By 1818, the AME

By the 1880s, Richard Allen's AME Church had spread as far south as Florida, where large congregations, such as the one pictured above, gathered for worship.

Church had a membership of nearly 8,000. The AME Church's members continued to exhibit their independent nature when, in the early 1820s, black Methodists in Wilmington, Delaware, and New York City had disagreements with Allen and left to establish their own independent congregations. Such activities by its membership would persist throughout Allen's years as head of the AME Church.

In 1823, Richard Allen faced a problem that was more personal in nature than the divisions in the church. Jonathan Tudas, a former Bethel member and founder of a rival congregation, distributed a leaflet accusing Allen of misusing church money. Tudas's accusations hurt Allen, who had not only worked for years without pay, but had also handled church expenses from his own personal income. (Throughout his ministry, Allen owned several successful businesses. This permitted him and his family to live comfortably in their own home without having to depend on earning an income from his work as a clergyman.) As always, Allen rose above the discord and went on with his endeavors.

In 1824, at the invitation of the Haitian president, a number of Bethel's members emigrated to the island nation of Haiti in the Caribbean. In an 1827 article that appeared in *Freedom's Journal*, the first newspaper in the United States published by blacks, Allen stated his opposition to this action. Pointing out that many former slaves could neither read nor write, he questioned whether these uneducated black immigrants could really educate the Haitian blacks, as they had been assigned to do.

Allen also opposed the idea of resettlement of freed blacks because he believed that their departure from the United States would be detrimental to the slaves who remained behind, for they would no longer have their freed brothers and sisters to serve as their role models. Instead, he urged reformers to concentrate on improving conditions for all black people in the United States and to continue to oppose slavery. "This land which we have watered with our tears and our blood is now our mother country and we are well satisfied to stay where wisdom abounds and the gospel is free," declared Allen. He also opened his home and Bethel African Church as havens for runaway slaves who were traveling north to freedom.

Three years after his article appeared, Allen presided at the organizational convention of the American Society of Free Persons of Color, which was held at Bethel. The goal of this new society was, first of all, to counteract the work of the American Colonization Society, a group that had been formed in Washington, D.C., in late 1816 to provide funds for the emigration of black people to Africa. In addition to their attempts to make life better for blacks who lived in the United States, the society also made plans to establish a community in Canada for blacks who needed to escape discrimination in the States.

At the time of his death on March 26, 1831, at age 71, Richard Allen was one of the leading black spokesmen in the United States and also the bishop of one of North America's first black denominations. Through his religious endeavors, he had helped his people for more than 50 years.

Sojourner Truth (1797?-1883), who was born Isabella Baumfree, chose her name because she believed that God had told her to travel and preach the truth.

2

Sojourner Truth
Standing Tall and Proud

*R*eflecting on her experiences and achievements, abolitionist and women's rights activist Sojourner Truth said of herself with pride, "I am the pure African." Truth stood almost six feet tall, and her arms were thick and muscular. For decades, this former slave traveled throughout the North, giving speeches to promote civil rights for blacks and women, supporting projects that would help blacks become economically secure, and teaching skills to newly freed blacks. Truth's tireless work for others often kept her separated from her family and left her on the brink of poverty.

Born a slave, Truth never learned to read or write. But she knew slavery was wrong and actively opposed it. In her years of speaking and public service, Truth became one of the most famous black women of the nineteenth century. Blacks and whites alike admired her fearlessness, and people repeated lines from her speeches and told anecdotes about her—from taking whites to court and rebuking racists to meeting with President Lincoln.

This legendary woman was born to James and Betsy (Mau-Mau Bett) Baumfree sometime between 1797 and 1800 in Ulster County, New York, the second youngest of 10 or 12 children. The Baumfree family was owned by a Dutch farmer named Johannes Hardenbergh. Because she was raised in a region that was settled by people of Dutch descent, Truth's first language was Dutch.

James and Betsy Baumfree named their baby daughter Isabella. While she was still a child, Isabella was sold away from her family and had several owners before she was a teenager. In 1810, Isabella Baumfree was purchased by John Dumont of New Paltz, New York, and would remain on his farm for the rest of her time as a slave. When she was about 19, she married an older slave named Tom, who also belonged to Dumont. They had five children: Diana, Peter, Elizabeth, Sophia, and James, who died when he was a young child.

The state of New York had decreed that all slaves were to be freed on July 4, 1827, but Dumont had promised to free Isabella's family one year before this emancipation law took effect. When this promised day came, however, Dumont refused to free Isabella and Tom and their children. Because of an injury to her hand, Isabella had been unable to work for him recently, so Dumont believed the family should stay with him longer. Angry at this broken promise, Isabella did some extra tasks to satisfy her own conscience and then left Dumont later that year. She took only the infant Sophia, and Tom and her other children remained at the Dumont place.

Isabella was never to reunite with her husband and would spend many years apart from her other children. She went to work in Hurley (about 12 miles away) for the family of Isaac Van Wagenen. In 1827, when her son Peter was sold into slavery in Alabama, Isabella Van Wagenen, as she was now called, went to court in nearby Kingston and successfully sued to have Peter returned to New York, where slavery was now illegal. Truth later recalled that when she began to fight to get her son back, she felt "as if the power of a nation was with me!"

During that same year, Isabella had an overwhelming spiritual experience. Her religious awakening led her to join a new Methodist church in Kingston, where she met a white schoolteacher from New York City. In 1829, the teacher brought Isabella and Peter to New York City and helped Isabella find employment as a maid. In the city, Isabella began attending the predominately white John Street Methodist Church. Later, she switched to the Zion Church, a black congregation.

Intensely religious, Isabella soon began preaching at camp meetings throughout the city. At one of these religious gatherings, she met Elijah Pierson, a white Baptist and self-styled preacher who had a loyal following called

Gathering to affirm their religious beliefs publicly was essential to most nineteenth-century blacks, including Isabella. Here a woman is baptized by immersion in a river.

the "Kingdom." With Pierson, Isabella did missionary work among New York City's prostitutes.

Not long after Isabella began working with Pierson, Matthias (or Robert Matthews), a white man whom Isabella would call "God on earth," introduced himself to the two missionaries. Matthias quickly succeeded Pierson as the Kingdom's religious leader. He claimed to have divine powers that allowed him to forgive sinners, punish the wicked, and heal the sick.

Isabella followed Matthias and lived at the Kingdom's commune in Sing Sing (now called Ossining), a town north of New York City, from 1832 to 1834. The only black member of the commune, Isabella cooked and cleaned for most of the group. She and the other members of the Kingdom had to obey Matthias's every order. He was a tyrant who demanded control over every aspect of his followers' lives and would whip them for even minor disobediences.

Matthias's Kingdom fell apart in 1834 after two former members, Benjamin and Ann Folger, accused Matthias of stealing. They also charged him and Isabella with murdering Elijah Pierson, who had died at the commune following an illness. Other former members claimed that the Kingdom's members had engaged in sex outside of marriage. Isabella stood by Matthias, who was acquitted of the murder charge. Then, for the second time in her life, Isabella took a white man to court when she sued Benjamin Folger for slandering her name. Although she won the case, she had given all her money to the Kingdom. She returned to New York City and for the next nine years again made her living as a maid.

In 1843, Isabella had another profound religious experience. She heard a voice telling her to travel around the United States and preach against greed, alcohol, and the sinfulness of city life. On June 1, 1843, Isabella Van Wagenen changed her name to Sojourner, which meant "wanderer." She later said that when she asked God for a new last name, she heard the word Truth, "because I was to declare the truth to the people." From then on, Isabella Van Wagenen was Sojourner Truth.

For months, Truth wandered throughout Long Island, New York, and up the Connecticut River Valley into Connecticut and Massachusetts. Along the way, she encountered a number of different religious groups, including the Millerites. They were the followers of William Miller, a preacher and farmer who predicted the end of the world would come in 1843. Because she believed in a loving God, Truth rejected the Millerites' doomsday message. Truth thought about becoming a member of the Shakers, a Christian group that believed that men and women were equal, that property should be owned communally, and that manual labor was a holy endeavor. Truth also considered joining Fruitlands, a well-known, though short-lived, utopian community in Harvard, Massachusetts, about 25 miles west of Boston.

Truth finally chose to live at the Northampton Association, a utopian colony that had been founded in 1842 in Northampton, Massachusetts, by a group that included abolitionists Samuel Hill and George Benson. Unlike most utopian communities of the period, which were farms, Northampton was a cooperatively run factory that manufactured silk. In this community, people strived to live in complete peace, equality, and harmony.

During her time at the Northampton Association, Truth became friends with renowned abolitionists such as William Lloyd Garrison, Frederick Douglass, and David Ruggles. After years of protecting fugitive slaves in New York City, Ruggles, who was going blind, had become a permanent resident at Northampton. Although the Northampton Association disbanded in 1846, for the next four years Truth continued to work as a servant for George Benson, one of the association's founders.

FREE LECTURE!

SOJOURNER TRUTH,

Although she never learned to read or write, Sojourner Truth became a powerful and popular speaker on the subjects of slavery and women's rights.

In 1850, Truth finally moved from gospel preaching to the reform speaking that would make her famous. That year, she made her first documented antislavery and women's rights speeches at conventions in New England. In 1851, William Lloyd Garrison urged her to join him on a lecture tour.

Like many black abolitionists of her day, Truth would publish an account of her life. She had dictated the *Narrative of Sojourner Truth* to Olive Gilbert in 1850. Truth sold the book on the lecture circuit and four years later was able to pay off the mortgage on the house she had purchased in Northampton, Massachusetts.

In 1850, Truth also became involved with the women's rights movement. Through her work, she met and befriended feminists such as Lucretia Mott and Elizabeth Cady Stanton and joined them in pursuing voting rights for all women.

In a legendary speech in May 1851, Sojourner Truth passionately defended women's rights at a convention in Akron, Ohio. Often called the "Ain't I a Woman?" speech, Truth's words there have become one of the most quoted pieces of oratory in American history. No complete version of Truth's speech was ever recorded, and in his biography, *Sojourner Truth: Slave, Prophet, Legend*, author Carleton Mabee warned that we should not assume that the version of the speech that has been handed down is actually what Truth said. The account that has gained fame was written by the convention chair, Frances Gage, 12 years later during the Civil War at a time when Truth had become extremely popular. Gage called her writing only "a faint sketch" of Truth's speech. But because Gage had attributed it to Sojourner Truth, the words have become Truth's.

Although it is not possible to know exactly what Sojourner Truth said that day in Akron, Gage recalled that her powerful message was the turning point of the

Harriet Beecher Stowe (1811-1896), author of the antislavery novel Uncle Tom's Cabin *(1852), made Sojourner Truth a legend by profiling her in the* Atlantic Monthly *magazine in 1863.*

convention. In the mid-1800s, many men argued that women should not have equal rights because they needed men's protection and because the Bible had claimed that it was Eve, the first woman, who had caused the fall of humankind from paradise. Truth, however, refuted such sexist arguments and, according to Gage, received thunderous applause from the mostly white audience.

Carleton Mabee described how the *Anti-Slavery Bugle* had reported Truth's speech. The newspaper stated that Truth had insisted that she should receive equal rights because "I am as strong as any man." According to the *Bugle*, Truth reasoned that if men think that a woman's intelligence is only the size of a pint while a man's is the size of a quart, "why can't she have her little pint full?"

For the rest of the decade, Truth spoke against slavery and for women's rights throughout the North. In her speeches, Truth talked about her own experience of slavery. She emphasized that slavery had left her ignorant and illiterate. Having aroused her audiences' sympathies, she then expressed pity for white slaveholders, who, she warned, would face God's judgment.

Truth's faith in God was always at the heart of her reform work. She had not left her religious pursuits to become a speaker for the rights of blacks and women; instead, it was her religion that drove her to speak out for those rights. One example of how her religion influenced her reform views was her reaction to an 1852 speech by the black abolitionist Frederick Douglass. When Douglass claimed that blacks could only gain freedom through violent struggle, Truth interrupted to ask, "Is God gone?" She firmly believed that God would not allow slavery to continue forever and, like many other antislavery activists, she opposed using violent means to end slavery. Instead of turning to violence, Truth trusted God and the essential goodness of human nature.

In 1857, Truth purchased a lot for a house in a religious community called Harmonia near Battle Creek, Michigan, where her three daughters and their families eventually joined her. Although Truth had promoted peaceful resistance to slavery, when the Civil War began in 1861, she praised the bravery of the Union soldiers. After black troops were allowed to join the Union army in 1863, Truth and her family worked to raise food for Thanksgiving dinners for the black soldiers.

In 1863, Truth traveled to Washington, D.C., to work with freed slaves. She met President Abraham Lincoln on October 29, 1864. On January 1, 1863, the president had signed the Emancipation Proclamation, which freed slaves in the Confederacy. Truth hoped that Lincoln would also grant freedom to the slaves living in the slave states of Missouri, Kentucky, Maryland, and Delaware that had remained loyal to the Union.

During the final years of the Civil War, Truth worked in Washington, D.C., with the federal government's Freedmen's Bureau. Although she held positions such as teacher of domestic skills, visitor, and distributor of supplies, she performed whatever work she felt needed to be done. In these roles, she helped out at the Freedmen's Hospital and also at the Freedmen's Village in Arlington, Virginia, across the Potomac River from the U.S. capital. The Freedmen's Bureau gave emergency aid to black refugees from slave states and provided medical treatment at no cost. While Truth was doing this work, she rode Washington's horse-drawn streetcars—which were reserved for white passengers—to protest segregation.

As she worked with the destitute free blacks in Washington, Truth became fearful that the refugees would become dependent on the government instead of learning how to earn money and make a living for themselves. After the Civil War ended, she became alarmed at the huge number of homeless blacks from the South. The Freedmen's Bureau was trying to place the former slaves in jobs in the North, but this was an expensive and

This painting commemorates the 1864 meeting between President Lincoln and Sojourner Truth.

slow process. So, in 1867, with the cooperation of friends in Battle Creek, Michigan, and Rochester, New York, Truth independently helped black people get jobs in these cities.

Truth knew, however, that the freed blacks also needed land on which to build their futures, so she petitioned the U.S. Congress to set aside parcels of western land for the former slaves. From 1870 to 1874, Truth traveled throughout the North, asking people to sign her petition. Although the government never allotted free land for blacks, in the late 1870s thousands of black families left southern states to escape persecution by whites. This exodus followed the 1877 departure of the federal troops that had been in the South since the end of the Civil War to protect the newly freed blacks. Many of these black pioneers settled in Kansas, where antislavery militants had won their own civil war in the 1850s, allowing Kansas to enter the Union as a free state in 1861. Truth and others hailed Kansas as a possible "Promised Land" in the blacks' "Exodus" from the South.

By the late 1870s, Truth's health had badly deteriorated. After several years of painful suffering, she died in Battle Creek on November 26, 1883, from infected sores on her legs, perhaps caused by diabetes.

Nearly 1,000 people from all over the United States attended Truth's funeral. In fact, hers was the largest funeral procession ever held in Battle Creek. Then, as now, the life and work of Sojourner Truth inspired the men and women who battled for equality for women and blacks in the United States.

This rough sketch is one of the few portraits that exist of the mysterious and controversial rebel, Nat Turner (1800–1831).

3

Nat Turner
Fiery Rebel

*W*hen Nat Turner led his insurrection in 1831, he became the most feared slave in the United States. Although this uprising failed and Turner was executed, his actions sparked unrest among U.S. slaves and helped to keep alive the hope that one day they would all be free.

Nat Turner was born on October 2, 1800, in Southampton County, Virginia, to slaves who were owned by Benjamin Turner. Nat Turner's father ran away when his son was eight or nine years old, so Nat was raised by his paternal grandmother, Old Bridget, and his mother, who was called Nancy. Nancy had arrived in Norfolk,

Virginia, in 1797 aboard a slave ship from Africa, and Benjamin Turner had bought her two years later. It was said that when Nat was born, his mother tried to kill him to save him from a life of slavery.

In the story of his life, *The Confessions of Nat Turner*, Nat recalled that when he was a child, his mother and grandmother believed he "was intended for some great purpose." Nat knew about events that had happened before his birth, and he had markings on his body that, according to his mother's native African religion, meant he was a prophet. Nat, too, believed he was destined for greatness, but he didn't know where or when or how.

When Nat was nine, Benjamin Turner sent him and his mother and grandmother to a nearby plantation owned by his son, Samuel. The following year Benjamin died and Nat's family became Samuel's property. Nat would spend the next 13 years on the Turner plantation.

For nearly as long as slavery had existed in the South, slaves had been attempting to overthrow their white masters. Eighty years before Nat Turner was born, in 1720, rebel slaves plotted to kill all the white people living in the Charleston, South Carolina, area and take over the city. Their plan, however, was discovered, and all of the conspirators were either burned, hanged, or deported.

Nineteen years later, in 1739, the first serious slave revolt in North America took place in the same region. In a year of unrest between slaves and their owners, a slave known as Jemmy led an uprising at Stono, located about 20 miles southwest of Charleston. In that insurrection, two warehouse guards were killed by a group of about 20

The fear of being sold at a slave auction, such as this one in Charleston, South Carolina, was one reason enslaved blacks rose up and killed their white masters.

rebelling slaves, who also stole guns and ammunition. Marching to the beat of drums and crying "Liberty!" the insurrectionists then headed south toward the Spanish colony of Florida, where they hoped to find refuge. Along the way, the band of rebels grew to nearly 80 as more and more slaves joined them, burning buildings and killing nearly all the white people they met. Eventually, many of the rebels were killed in several battles with the militia, and most of those who fled were later caught and executed. In all, the Stono Rebellion resulted in the deaths of an estimated 25 whites and 50 slaves.

More terrifying to whites were the revolts by black Haitians in the Caribbean, including their 1801 conquest of Santo Domingo (now the Dominican Republic). The Haitian revolutionaries had ended slavery and won independence from France. In 1801, their first government was established under Toussaint L'Ouverture, a former slave. Among southern whites in the 1800s, "Remember Santo Domingo!" would be the warning cry whenever revolts occurred or abolitionists agitated against slavery.

As a boy growing up in rural Virginia, Nat Turner no doubt heard stories about slave rebellions. In 1800, the year in which he and another future rebel, John Brown, were born, a slave named Gabriel planned a massive

John Brown (1800-1859), a white man, led his own rebellion against the institution of slavery when he and 21 followers took control of the federal arsenal at Harpers Ferry, Virginia, in 1859. Like Nat Turner, Brown became a legendary hero to many blacks.

insurrection involving thousands of slaves living in the Richmond, Virginia, area. The organizers of the conspiracy vowed to spare white Methodists and Quakers, members of two religious groups that opposed slavery, as well as people of French descent. (Gabriel thought the United States had declared war on France and, therefore, believed that the French might aid the rebels.) They hoped that poor whites would also join their rebellion.

The insurrection failed, however, because two slaves revealed the plan. Then a storm prevented the approximately 1,000 armed slaves who had gathered six miles outside of Richmond from crossing the marsh that separated them from the city. When none of the rebels who had been arrested would give any information to the authorities, their courage prompted one observer to warn that if other slaves had their "sense of their rights, and contempt of danger, and a thirst for revenge," then they might "deluge the Southern country in blood." Gabriel and 15 other would-be insurrectionists were hanged on October 7, 1800, and about 20 more were hanged later.

On May 30, 1822, former slave Denmark Vesey organized yet another slave revolt in Charleston, South Carolina. But, tipped off by frightened blacks, white slave owners arrested Vesey and his approximately 130 followers before they could carry out their revolt. Neither Vesey nor any of the other 36 rebels who were hanged ever revealed any information about their plan. Twelve other participants were sent to a penal colony.

Nat Turner's owner died that same year, so 22-year-old Nat, along with his wife, Cherry, and their children, were put up for sale. Thomas Moore purchased Nat for $400, and Cherry and their children were sold to Moore's neighbor, Giles Reese.

Believing he "was ordained for some great purpose in the hands of the Almighty," Turner began preaching to other slaves in 1825. His sermons described a coming day of judgment when "white spirits and black spirits engaged in battle." Thomas Moore did not interfere with his preaching because he considered Turner hard-working and trustworthy. His reputation as a prophet and healer continued to grow, even among some whites in the area.

In 1826 (some records say 1827) Nat Turner ran away from the Moore farm after Moore had hired an abusive overseer. Before he returned to the farm, Nat spent 30 days hiding in the nearby woods. During that time, he heard a voice demanding, "Seek ye the Kingdom of Heaven." This he interpreted as a call to freedom.

In May 1828, Turner had a vision that told him to "arise and prepare myself, and slay my enemies with their own weapons." Later that month, voices told him that "the time was fast approaching when the first should be last and the last should be first." (Thomas Moore died later that year. In 1830, Moore's widow remarried, and her new husband, Joseph Travis, became Turner's new master.)

Turner finally saw the sign for action in February 1831, when an eclipse of the sun occurred. To many people, both black and white, this meant the end of the world was near. For Turner, it was an omen that showed the time for a slave rebellion was now at hand.

Turner shared his plan with six trusted friends and his wife, Cherry, who kept his maps and other papers in her cabin. They planned their revolt for the Fourth of July because a holiday would be a lighter work day for slaves and a time when they would be allowed to move about the community more freely. Furthermore, whites would be busy celebrating with their families and friends and, therefore, would be more apt to be taken by surprise. But Turner became ill on July 4, so he had to postpone the uprising.

On August 13, the sun shimmered a strange, bluish-green color, and then a black spot appeared on its surface. To Turner, this was the sign he had been waiting for. He met with his followers on August 21 to make the final plans for their campaign of terror. "Just as the black spot passed over the sun, so shall the blacks pass over the earth," he declared, maintaining that killing every white person in the area was the slaves' only chance for freedom.

The uprising began shortly after midnight on August 22, 1831, when Nat and four of his men met at Cabin Pond on the Reese farm, where Cherry lived. Returning to the Travis farm, they were joined by the other rebels. Nat used a ladder to climb into a window of the Travis house, and he then came downstairs to let the others in. In his *Confessions,* Turner recounted what happened after he had stolen his master's guns:

> It was then observed that I must spill first blood. Armed with a hatchet and accompanied by Will, I entered my master's chamber. It being dark, I could not give him a death blow: the hatchet glanced from his head, he sprang

from the bed and called to his wife. It was his last word—Will laid him dead with a blow of his ax, and Mrs. Travis shared the same fate as she lay in the bed.

After leading the first attack, Turner kept to the rear of the group, carrying a blunt sword and directing the action. He would slay only one of the victims.

Turner and his band killed six people at the Travis farm. They then surprised and attacked several other slaveholders, including six more on three neighboring farms. At every farm, more blacks joined the group. By

HORRID MASSACRE IN VIRGINIA

This woodcut from the time depicts Turner's rebellion. The original caption describes (1) "a Mother intreating for the lives of her children" and (2) "Mr. Travis, cruelly murdered by his own Slaves."

*The house of Giles Reese, who owned Nat Turner's
wife, Cherry. Turner and his group of rebels spared
the Reese family in their path of destruction.*

noon, about 60 slaves were a part of the insurrection, rid-
ing their owners' horses and armed with their owners'
guns and knives. Before their revolt was put down,
Turner and his fellow slaves had killed at least 57 white
people, including infants and older children, men and
women. Although it had not been their original plan,
they decided to spare the lives of several white families,
including those of Giles Reese, Cherry's owner; John
Clark Turner, Samuel Turner's son and Nat's childhood
friend; and a poor white neighbor who owned no slaves.

By early afternoon, the rebels had lost their advantage of surprise. A slave from the Travis farm had ridden

to warn Travis's brother-in-law, Nathaniel Francis, about the uprising, and Francis quickly rode into the nearby town of Jerusalem, where several local militia units were then organized. The town's officials also sought assistance from state and federal military organizations, and a total of 3,000 armed men were sent to the area.

Turner's group of rebels had their first skirmishes with the militia later that afternoon. The newer recruits from the neighboring farmsteads were not as committed and trustworthy as were the members of Turner's original band. Many of them were drunk from drinking the liquor they had stolen and had become difficult to control. The morning of August 23 found the group panicked and divided, as well as exhausted from lack of sleep, drinking too much alcohol, and battles with the militia. They also lacked guns and ammunition because they had not been able to take over the town of Jerusalem.

By now, some of the rebel slaves had been killed or captured by the militia and others had deserted. Those who were caught were tortured and forced to provide information about the identities of their fellow rebels and any plans for more assaults. Although most of the slaves had been taken during the first few days of the uprising, Turner escaped and hid in a hole he had dug in a field near the Travis farm. The authorities beat and tortured Cherry while her husband was in hiding to try to find out where he was.

As a result of widespread rumors about new insurrection plots and approaching armies of slaves, fearful whites fled or hid and also began torturing and killing innocent slaves and free blacks throughout the South. In Southampton County, Virginia, and the neighboring North Carolina counties, more than 120 blacks were killed because they were suspected of having taken part in Turner's insurrection.

Before Nat Turner was captured, 50 rebels had stood trial. About 20 were hanged and many others were eventually sold to slaveholders who lived farther south. When Turner had not been found after two months, some thought he had escaped to the Caribbean. Others believed he was still somewhere in the South, secretly inciting more insurrectionist activities among black slaves.

Turner lived in several hiding places for over two months, sneaking out at night for food and water. On October 30, 1831, he was finally captured. While Turner was in jail awaiting trial, Thomas Gray, a young lawyer, interviewed him. The result was a remarkable document, *The Confessions of Nat Turner*, which recounted the story of Turner's life from his childhood prophesies to his insurrection and capture. Although some have questioned the reliability of the memoirs because they were recorded by Gray and not written by Turner (although Turner could read and write), they remain a powerful account of his religious beliefs and his plans for the rebellion. When Gray asked him whether he had been mistaken in his belief that God had called him to lead the insurrection, Turner replied, "Was not Christ crucified?"

At his November 5 trial, Nat Turner pleaded "Not guilty" because he felt no guilt for his actions. At the trial and also in his *Confessions*, he identified only those rebels

53

Nat Turner spent several weeks hiding in the woods before he was discovered by a local farmer named Benjamin Phipps, who delivered Turner to the authorities at gunpoint.

who had already been killed. Found guilty, Turner was hanged on November 11, 1831. After Turner's death, Giles Reese sold Cherry and her daughter to a slave-owner who lived in another state.

For years following Nat Turner's insurrection, slaves and free blacks were terrorized and often killed in order to frighten other potential rebels into submission. Because Turner and many of his co-conspirators had seemed to be loyal slaves, southern slaveholders began to fear all of their slaves. Harsher and more widespread laws regulating the activities of both slaves and free blacks were passed. Throughout the South, it was now illegal to teach slaves how to read, and in some places even selling pamphlets or pencils to slaves was against the law. Blacks were forbidden to hold religious meetings or other gatherings in many regions because slaveowners suspected that they used these services to incite and plan revolts. Whites tried to keep track of their slaves at all times, and a slave caught out at night without a pass would be whipped by white patrols.

For many slaves and free blacks, however, Nat Turner's rebellion remained a powerful cry for freedom, and Turner was seen as a hero. Some later abolitionists considered him to be a martyr for their cause and they warned that unless slavery was brought to an end there would be more rebellions such as his. In the decades following the insurrection, antislavery activists began to accept that the institution would not end peacefully. Violence over the issue of slavery in Kansas and Missouri in the 1850s and John Brown's attack on Harpers Ferry in 1859 demonstrated that the nation was finally heading for the battle against slavery that Nat Turner had died trying to win.

Henry Highland Garnet (1815-1882), a Presbyterian minister, was an outspoken radical who called upon slaves to slay their owners.

4

Henry Highland Garnet
Preaching Resistance

*H*enry Highland Garnet rose from slavery to become a nationally recognized abolitionist and diplomat. He is, however, best remembered for his speech at the National Negro Convention in Buffalo, New York, in 1843. At that convention, he addressed blacks who had gathered from around the nation to discuss strategies for ending slavery and advancing the rights of free blacks. In his speech, "An Address to the Slaves of the United States of America" (sometimes called "Call to Rebellion"), he told black people that they "must themselves strike the blow" against slavery by whatever means necessary. Although there had been a number of earlier slave rebellions in the United States, this was the first time that a black man had publicly called for a widespread, planned revolt.

On December 23, 1815, Henry Highland Garnet was born to George and Hennie, who were slaves on the William Spencer plantation near New Market, Maryland. He was said to have been the grandson of a ruler of the Mandingo empire in West Africa.

In 1824, when Henry was nine, his master died. Taking advantage of this situation, Henry's father began planning his family's escape to the North. He obtained the traveling passes that slaves needed to show whenever they were away from their home plantation, saying he was taking his family to their deceased master's funeral. Instead, when Henry's family left the Spencer plantation in a covered wagon, they began their journey to freedom.

Along with their children, Henry and Mary, and several other slaves, George and Hennie traveled by wagon and on foot from Maryland into Delaware. In Wilmington, George sought out Thomas Garrett, a Quaker who helped many slaves make their way to freedom. Garrett's house was the family's first stop on the Underground Railroad—a collection of safe hiding places along a route established by abolitionists for blacks escaping from the South to new homes in the free northern states or in Canada. Because Delaware was still a slave state, Garrett arranged for Henry's family to travel farther north to the free state of Pennsylvania. The family, however, continued on to New York City, arriving there in 1825. In New York, George worked as a shoemaker and

Like many slaves who escaped to the free states in the North, Henry Highland Garnet and his family were helped by the Underground Railroad.

became active in the African Methodist Episcopal Church. As was the custom to show that they were no longer living as slaves, George renamed his wife and his daughter—they would now be known as Elizabeth and Eliza—and he took the surname of Garnet.

On July 4, 1827, some two years after the Garnet family had come to New York City, the state of New York abolished slavery. On the following day, the Garnets joined the large group of jubilant blacks who crowded the streets to celebrate Emancipation Day. No doubt seeing so many black people rejoicing in their freedom and expressing pride in their African heritage left a lasting impression on 11-year-old Henry. At the time, he was a student at the New York African Free School, which had been established in 1787 by the New York Manumission Society, an abolitionist group, to educate gifted young black boys. Henry would spend two years at the school before leaving to work as a cabin boy on a boat that sailed a route between New York City and Washington, D.C.

Although slavery had been abolished in the state of New York, the federal fugitive slave laws of 1793 still permitted southern slaveowners to apprehend runaway slaves who were residing in free states and transport them back to the slave states from which they had escaped. To track down and recapture fugitives, or escaped slaves, whom they believed were still rightfully theirs, slaveowners would sometimes hire slave catchers.

It was in 1829, while Henry was away working on the sailing ship, that a relative of the family's former master came to the Garnet home, accompanied by a group of slave hunters. When George Garnet heard the relative ask for him, he recognized his voice and escaped by jumping out of an upper-story window. Some neighbors hid his wife, so she also managed to evade the men, but their daughter, Eliza, was taken captive. She was later released when she persuaded the authorities that she had never lived in the South and, therefore, was not a runaway.

When Henry returned to New York City, he found the family's home destroyed and learned that, fearing the slave catchers' return, his family had separated and fled to

Fugitive slave laws made it legal for slave owners to pursue and capture escaped slaves—even in the free northern states.

various sections of nearby Long Island. He was so angry that he bought a large knife and spent days walking the streets of New York, searching for the slave hunters.

Now all alone, with no home and his family missing, Henry went to work on a Long Island farm. His quick wit and intelligence so impressed the farm family's son that he began to tutor Henry. At the farm, the 14-year-old injured his leg while playing a game. The leg would trouble Henry for years before it was finally amputated.

After three years, Garnet returned New York City to join his reunited family and to resume his education. Compared to many other young black men of the time, Henry Garnet was well educated. Among his fellow students at the New York African Free School were several other talented young men who would later become famous, including Alexander Crummell, whose family lived next door to the Garnets and who would become a renowned minister; a fellow antislavery speaker and writer, Samuel Ringgold Ward, who was Garnet's cousin; and Ira Aldridge, an internationally known Shakespearean actor. Garnet then studied Latin and Greek at a new city high school for blacks.

After their graduation, Garnet and his classmates Alexander Crummell and Thomas Sidney were invited to continue their studies at the Noyes Academy, another school that had been established by an antislavery society. The journey to Canaan, New Hampshire, about 400 miles north of New York City, was a difficult one because hotels refused to rent rooms to the young men or provide them with food because they were black. When they traveled by steamboat or stagecoach, they were not permitted to sit inside; instead, they had to ride on top, exposed to all kinds of weather. Garnet's lame leg also caused him pain.

Although they were warmly received when they finally arrived at the school in July 1835, a large group of white farmers objected to blacks having the opportunity to receive an education. The following month, the farmers hitched together many teams of oxen and used them to drag the school building off its foundation and into a nearby swamp. When the white mob began shooting at the students, 19-year-old Garnet led his classmates in returning their fire. Soon afterwards, however, Garnet and 11 other black students left Noyes. As they drove away in a wagon, the enraged farmers fired a cannon at them.

Then, in 1836, Garnet began three years of study at the Oneida Theological Institute, a seminary near Whitesboro, New York. One of his teachers at the school was Beriah Green, a white abolitionist who believed blacks had the ability to excel academically. During the celebration of the American Anti-Slavery Society's seventh anniversary in 1840, Green arranged for Garnet to speak to the group on the subject of slavery. His remarks were well received, and Garnet began to realize that some white people could be his allies.

After graduating from Oneida, Garnet moved to Troy, New York, to teach at a school for blacks. In 1842, he was licensed to preach and the following year was ordained as the pastor of the Liberty Street Presbyterian Church, the only black Presbyterian church in New York.

Being a minister gave Henry Garnet a platform from which he could express his opinions about the evils of slavery and tell his listeners what they could do to help to bring about its end. In addition to speaking out from the pulpit, he frequently wrote articles for the *Colored American*, a black activist newspaper that had been established in 1837. In his antislavery endeavors, he was often assisted by Julia Williams, an educated black woman whom he had married in 1841.

Sometimes Garnet also spoke on behalf of the American Anti-Slavery Society, the organization that had been established by William Lloyd Garrison in 1833. Garrison and his followers, often called "Garrisonians," believed in abolishing slavery through persuasion or what they called "moral suasion." Unlike some other abolitionists, they did not favor using political means to bring about change, and they especially opposed violence. Instead, the Garrisonians hoped that by giving lectures and publishing pamphlets and newspapers they could convince slaveholders that they were evil and that slavery was a sinful institution.

Garnet, however, gradually came to support the use of political action. He maintained that because most state and national governmental bodies were composed of white people, blacks needed to secure their aid to bring about any change. But he was also convinced that because only black people could truly understand their struggle, they would ultimately have to fight alone in order to attain their freedom. He also believed that only through the use of violence could slaves end their enslavement. (Shortly after moving to Troy, he had even envisioned organizing a widespread revolt in the South, but his bad leg had prevented him from traveling. After the leg became worse, it was finally amputated in 1840.)

In 1843, the year of his ordination as a pastor, Garnet delivered his now-famous speech at the National Negro Convention in Buffalo, New York. Garnet's powerful "Call to Rebellion" moved many in the audience:

> You had far better all *die—die immediately*, than live slaves, and entail your wretchedness upon your posterity. If you would be free in this generation, here is your only hope. . . . Brethren, arise, arise! Strike for your lives and liberties. Now is the day and the hour. Let every slave

"SLAVERY!" Henry Highland Garnet exclaimed in his fiery 1843 speech, "How much misery is comprehended in that single word."

throughout the land do this, and the days of slavery are numbered. You cannot be more oppressed than you have been—you cannot suffer greater cruelties than you have already. *Rather die freemen than live to be slaves. . . .* Let your motto be resistance! *resistance!* RESISTANCE! No oppressed people have ever secured their liberty without resistance.

In his speech at the same meeting, fellow abolitionist Frederick Douglass took issue with Garnet's militant stance. It was very likely that his opposition influenced the assembled delegates to miss passing Garnet's resolution for rebellion by only one vote.

Four years later, in 1847, at another National Negro Convention, this time held at Garnet's church in Troy, his previous resolution was resubmitted and unanimously passed. But because Garnet was unable to generate widespread support, his plans did not move forward.

Garnet's next important political appearance was in 1850 when he served as a delegate to the World Peace Congress in Frankfurt, Germany. Afterwards, he traveled throughout Europe, lecturing to various antislavery groups. He so impressed the United Presbyterian Church of Scotland that they asked him to go to Jamaica, a British colony in the West Indies, as a missionary and teacher. In 1852, Garnet became pastor of a congregation in the village of Stirling, Grange Hill, in Jamaica. He stayed there for four years but then had to return to the United States in 1856 because of illness.

When Garnet recovered, he served as pastor of Shiloh Presbyterian Church in New York City and began to encourage U.S. blacks to emigrate to Jamaica. Although Frederick Douglass still opposed his ideas, Garnet's views were being embraced by a number of black leaders, including Martin Delany, with whom he founded the African Civilization Society in 1858. Their society hoped to end slavery by encouraging U.S. blacks to resettle in Africa to grow cotton. The competition with the South's most profitable crop, they reasoned, would eventually eliminate the need for southern slavery.

At the start of the Civil War in 1861, Garnet returned to England. Once again, he spoke out against the practice of slavery in the southern states that were now united against the federal government as the Confederacy. In England, there were many Confederate sympathizers because the southern states provided the cotton they needed for their textile mills. Garnet knew that keeping Britain out of the war and preventing its ships from entering Confederate ports would seriously damage the southern economy and, thus, would help the North win the war. After returning to the States, Garnet helped to recruit black soldiers for the Union army.

On January 31, 1865, after months of debate and compromise, the U.S. Congress passed what would become the Thirteenth Amendment that abolished slavery. To commemorate the event, President Abraham Lincoln asked Garnet, who the previous year had moved to Washington to take a new church position, to give a sermon to the U.S. House of Representatives. Garnet's powerful words of February 12, 1865, denounced the "fearful national sin" of slavery and called for freedom and equality for all blacks. "Favored men," he said to the assembled lawmakers, "speedily finish the work which he [President Lincoln] has given you to do. Emancipate, Enfranchise, Educate, and Give the blessings of the gospel to every American citizen." Garnet was the first black clergyman ever to preach in the Capitol, and his speech was widely printed in newspapers throughout the country.

When Garnet traveled in the South following the war—he even returned to the boyhood home from which he had escaped at the age of nine—he was dismayed with what he saw. Garnet wanted blacks to have their own land, but this was not happening. In fact, many southern states had passed new laws that effectively restricted black people from owning property.

Garnet continued to speak out for equality for black people after returning to Washington. He criticized the unsuccessful efforts of President Andrew Johnson's Reconstruction government to guarantee black equality, and he continued to preach that black people could rise in society only by becoming economically independent. They were not discriminated against by white people because of their skin color, he declared. Instead, they suffered prejudice because they were poor and uneducated. When former slaves were able to earn a salary, they would be able to purchase property. Having property of their own would lead to financial freedom. And financial freedom, Garnet said, would eventually bring them equality with whites. "You know it is better [to] work for Mr. Cash than Mr. Lash [a slave master]," Garnet told blacks. "The more money you make, the lighter your skin will be. The more land and houses you get, the straighter your hair will be."

As Garnet grew increasingly frustrated when black people remained poor and subject to discrimination long after the Civil War had ended, he became convinced that U.S. blacks would never be able to achieve full equality with whites. Therefore, he continued to urge black people to emigrate to Jamaica and Haiti or return to Africa, where he believed they could finally live as free citizens.

In June 1881, Henry Garnet became a diplomat to the West African nation of Liberia, a country that the American Colonization Society had helped to establish in

Noted statesman Henry Clay (1777-1852) was a prominent supporter of the American Colonization Society, which sought to return free blacks to Africa. Henry Highland Garnet's African Civilization Society countered this organization by promoting voluntary emigration for blacks.

1822 as a permanent home for freed U.S. slaves. Garnet died there on February 13, 1882, and, according to his wishes, was buried in Africa, the homeland of his royal ancestors.

Henry Highland Garnet's ideas, radical in his day, have endured and given life to the civil-rights struggles of the twentieth century. More than 100 years after Garnet's famous speech calling for blacks to resist oppression violently, the black nationalist and spiritual leader Malcolm X would tell his followers that they, too, must secure their social and political freedom "by any means necessary."

Frederick Douglass (1818-1895), the most famous black man of his day, escaped slavery to become a noted abolitionist, author, journalist, orator, and statesman.

5

Frederick Douglass
Eloquent Crusader

*O*n August 12, 1841, the Massachusetts Anti-Slavery Society gathered in a meeting hall on Nantucket, an island off the Massachusetts coast. After several well-known white antislavery speakers, including William Lloyd Garrison and Wendell Phillips, had finished their speeches, a tall, handsome black man hesitantly stood up and began to talk about his life as a slave. His eloquent words and powerful delivery would make Frederick Douglass not only one of the most popular speakers of the antislavery movement but also one of the nineteenth century's most renowned orators.

William Lloyd Garrison (1805-1879) published the Liberator, *an abolitionist newspaper, from 1831 to 1865. Frederick Douglass considered this newspaper second only to the Bible in its importance to his life.*

Douglass was born Frederick Augustus Bailey in 1818 in Talbot County, Maryland. His mother was a slave named Harriet Bailey. Although Frederick never knew who his father was, he suspected him to be his master, Captain Aaron Anthony, who managed a plantation for the wealthy Lloyd family.

While still an infant, Frederick was sent to stay with his grandparents on another plantation about 12 miles away. In 1824, when he was six, Frederick was taken back to the Lloyd plantation, where he lived in the Anthony home, apart from his mother, who died shortly afterward. He was cared for by the overbearing slave cook, whom Frederick called Aunt Katy. To punish him for misbehaving, Aunt Katy often refused to give him any food.

Also residing at the Anthony home were Captain Anthony's daughter Lucretia and her husband, Thomas Auld. Lucretia took a special liking to Frederick (who may have been her half brother) and protected him from Aunt Katy. When Anthony became ill in 1826, he left his position as manager of the Lloyd plantation and moved with his own slaves to one of his farms in Tuckahoe, Maryland. Lucretia and Thomas, however, arranged for Frederick to go to Baltimore to live with Thomas's brother and sister-in-law, Hugh and Sophia Auld.

The Aulds treated eight-year-old Frederick more like a member of their family than a slave. He was not required to do any hard work but was responsible for watching over their young son, Tommy. Even so, Frederick was always aware that he was not free.

In October 1827, Frederick was brought back to Tuckahoe. Captain Anthony had died the previous November, and now his slaves were to be divided among his children. Although most of Frederick's family went to Anthony's sons, Thomas Auld became Frederick's new master and, once again, sent the young Frederick to live in Baltimore. He would remain there for five years.

Because Frederick was extremely bright, Sophia began to teach him how to read, using the family Bible. Their lessons ended abruptly when Frederick attempted to read for Hugh Auld. Auld warned his wife that "learning would spoil the best [slave] in the world."

Auld's reaction made Frederick realize that reading must be a powerful asset. So, with Tommy's *Webster's Spelling Book*, he secretly continued to teach himself to read. He also bought a copy of *The Columbian Orator* and began to learn the words of the world's greatest speeches. One of the orations, "Dialogue between Master and Slave," helped Frederick understand the importance of freedom and the meaning of the talk about abolition that he had overheard on Baltimore's streets.

Frederick was also influenced by Dr. Lewis G. Wells, a black physician and lecturer, whom he had first heard at Baltimore's Dallas Street Methodist Church. Frederick began teaching Sunday classes and, after meeting several preachers, had a religious conversion that led him to believe his life was destined for greatness.

Fearing that the freedom Frederick had might lead him to run away, the Aulds returned him to live with Thomas Auld and his new wife, Rowena, when he was 14. (Lucretia had died in 1826.) His new masters expected him to be obedient, and they punished him by starving him when he refused to follow their orders.

One activity the Aulds thought was not proper for a slave was teaching Sunday school. One Sunday, Auld and a number of his fellow white Methodists interrupted Frederick's class, clubs in hand, demanding to know whether he "wanted to be another Nat Turner." This incident put an end to his teaching.

After nine months of trying to change Frederick's behavior, Thomas Auld hired him out to Edward Covey. Covey was a farmer with a reputation for "breaking" slaves—for working them so hard that they eventually lost their spirit to resist. From January 1, 1833, until the late summer, Frederick toiled in Covey's fields from morning till night in all kinds of weather. After a life-threatening beating, Frederick fled to the Aulds, but he was forced to return to the Covey farm when Thomas Auld was not sympathetic to his complaints and even laughed when he said that Covey would kill him.

On the way back to the farm, Frederick met Sandy Jenkins, a free black man, who gave him a "magic" root that he claimed would protect Frederick from Covey. A few days later, when Covey grabbed Frederick and attempted to tie him up to whip him, Frederick unexpectedly struck back. In the autobiography of his life as a slave, *Narrative of the Life of Frederick Douglass*, he marvelled that "from whence came the spirit I don't know— I resolved to fight."

Covey and the young man struggled for nearly two hours. Afterwards, Frederick recalled that the fight had "rekindled [in him] the few expiring embers of freedom, and revived within me a sense of my own manhood. . . . However long I might remain a slave in form, the day had passed forever when I could be a slave in fact." Perhaps Covey, too, had recognized the change in Frederick, for he never hit the young slave again.

Frederick's time with Covey ended on Christmas Day, 1833. On New Year's Day, Auld sent him to work for William Freeland. Life on the Freeland farm was easier for Frederick because he was no longer beaten. Frederick became close friends with the other slaves at the Freeland place and on the neighboring farms. He also started a Sunday school and secretly taught about two dozen young black men how to read and write. This was a dangerous undertaking for Frederick and his students, for they risked severe punishment if they were caught.

In spite of being treated relatively well by William Freeland, Frederick was becoming more and more discontented with life as a slave. In 1835, he and some of his friends began to devise an escape plan. Taking a canoe that belonged to a white neighbor, they intended to leave the night before Easter and paddle 70 miles up the Chesapeake Bay. Then they would follow the North Star until they reached freedom in Pennsylvania. Frederick had the task of preparing the passes they would need to show if they were stopped along the way.

Their plans fell through, however. Sandy Jenkins, who had backed out of the trip, betrayed the others. When the rest of the group were arrested on the Saturday they were going to leave, they managed to destroy their forged passes—Frederick threw his into a fire, and the others ate theirs on the way to jail—so the authorities had no solid evidence of any escape plan. Everyone else was soon released, but Frederick was held for another week and was threatened with execution or being sold far into the South. Thomas Auld, however, had him released and returned him to the Aulds in Baltimore.

Back in Baltimore, 17-year-old Frederick was hired out as an apprentice caulker for a shipyard. (Caulkers cover a ship's seams to make the vessel watertight.) There he suffered insults and threats from white workers who did not want to work with black people. Frederick left the shipyard after a severe beating by fellow workers and, in May 1838, convinced Hugh Auld to let him find his own work. In exchange for being allowed to live on his own, he would pay Auld $3 every week. Auld also promised that Douglass could purchase his freedom at age 25.

Frederick now became involved with Baltimore's large population of free blacks. Although the church was at the center of this community, Frederick, who had lost the religious fervor of his youth, instead chose to join the East Baltimore Mental Improvement Society, a group that met secretly to engage in formal debates. Among the free blacks whom Frederick met was his future wife, Anna Murray, who was employed as a maid.

After Hugh Auld made him return to his home in late summer, Frederick began making plans to escape and

Frederick, obsessed with discovering his birthdate, believed that he might have been born on February 14 because his mother had called him "Valentine" in 1825 during one of her last visits with him.

to marry Anna. For several months, he had tasted freedom and had worked for wages. Now he could no longer endure living as a slave.

It was probably the sale of Anna's featherbed that provided the funds for Frederick's escape. Dressed in a sailor's uniform (that Anna had reportedly sewn) and carrying the identification papers he had borrowed from a free black sailor he had known at the shipyard, Frederick boarded a train on September 3, 1838, that was leaving for Wilmington, Delaware. Fortunately, the conductor didn't examine his documents too closely.

After journeying many terror-filled hours on trains and ferries, Frederick finally arrived in New York City. Even with no food and no place to stay, Frederick finally felt like a free man. He had "a free state around me, and free earth under my feet!" But when Frederick encountered a former slave he had once known, the freed man told him to trust no one with his secret of having escaped slavery. For a few dollars, he was told, black spies would turn him over to the slave catchers.

Early the next morning, however, Frederick met a sailor whom he immediately trusted. The man took him to the home of David Ruggles, a free black who was a conductor on the Underground Railroad. He stayed with Ruggles until Anna joined him and they were married.

After their marriage, Ruggles sent the couple to New Bedford, Massachusetts, a largely Quaker seaport town, where they stayed with a free black couple, Nathan and Mary Johnson. At Ruggles's suggestion, Frederick had given up his last name to avoid being easily traced.

David Ruggles had arranged for two Quakers,
William C. Taber and Joseph Ricketson, to escort the
newly married Frederick and Anna to New Bedford.

When he discovered that "Johnson," the name he had taken in New York City, was too commonplace in New Bedford, he chose the last name of "Douglass" from a novel he had read. Now he was no longer Frederick Bailey, slave, but Frederick Douglass, free man.

In New Bedford, Douglass failed to secure employment as a ship's caulker because he was black. Instead, he worked a variety of menial jobs, from chopping wood to loading ships. He became more involved in the black community, attending antislavery meetings and joining the African Methodist Episcopal Zion Church.

Nine months after their marriage, Anna gave birth to their first child, Rosetta. Lewis Henry was born in

1840, and three more children followed: Frederick Jr. in 1842, Charles Remond in 1844, and Annie in 1849.

It was in New Bedford that Douglass first read William Lloyd Garrison's antislavery newspaper, the *Liberator*. Douglass called the newspaper "my meat and drink," and Garrison became Douglass's hero—a "Moses" who would "deliver His modern Israel from bondage."

Garrison was one of the leaders of the 1841 gathering of more than 1,000 antislavery activists in Nantucket. This was the first time Douglass had heard Garrison speak. Three days later, on August 12, Douglass made his first public appearance before the same group and made a huge impression on the audience. After he spoke, John A. Collins, an agent for the Massachusetts Anti-Slavery Society, invited Douglass to represent their national organization. For the next 10 years, Douglass would travel throughout the northern and midwestern states, speaking on behalf of Garrison's American Anti-Slavery Society.

Garrison and his followers believed that the free states should break apart from the slave states. In their view, the Constitution was evil because it permitted slavery. Douglass accepted this opinion and also supported the Garrisonians' nonviolent methods for achieving change, as well as their belief in equal rights for women.

Although Douglass was at first primarily involved in the mostly white American Anti-Slavery Society, he would also become active in the work of black-led organizations. At the National Negro Convention in Buffalo, New York, in 1843, the more moderate Garrisonian beliefs of Douglass clashed with those of another black leader, Henry Highland Garnet, and led him to oppose Garnet's support of a resolution endorsing a slave revolt.

Douglass drew large crowds wherever he appeared. When he stepped to the platform, Garrison would introduce him as "a piece of southern property who had become a man." Referring to the beatings that Douglass suffered as a slave, John Collins, the man who had recruited him in Massachusetts, would tell audiences that Douglass had graduated from the institution of slavery "with his diploma written on his back."

Because he spoke so well, some people doubted that Douglass had ever been a slave. It was to end those rumors that he decided to write his life story. Published in 1845, *Narrative of the Life of Frederick Douglass* was praised by readers everywhere and is still read today. Douglass would later write two more autobiographies, *My Bondage and My Freedom* (1855) and *The Life and Times of Frederick Douglass* (1881).

Along with Douglass's growing fame on the lecture circuit came the increased danger of his being found by the Aulds. To remain safe following the publication of his book in 1845, Douglass left on a two-year tour of Great Britain. Traveling in Ireland, Scotland, and England, he spoke out not only against slavery in America, but also against the mistreatment of native peoples of the British colonies throughout the world as well as the oppression of working people everywhere. Huge crowds flocked to his speeches, and he sold thousands of copies of his book.

Because Douglass had not experienced any racism in Great Britain, he considered moving there permanently.

It proved impossible for him to move his family to England, however, and he eventually needed to go home. To guarantee his safety, Douglass's English friends raised the $1,250 that was needed to purchase his freedom from Thomas Auld. They also gave him money to start an antislavery newspaper. On November 30, 1846, Frederick Douglass legally became a free man.

While in England, Douglass had begun to distance himself from Garrison's American Anti-Slavery Society because he wanted to follow his own antislavery pursuits. He was also eager to work more closely with other black abolitionists. "We must be our own representatives and advocates," he stated. Many of his former associates were critical of his starting his own newspaper because they feared the competition would hurt Garrison's *Liberator*, which was struggling financially.

Soon after returning to the United States in 1847, Douglass moved his family from Massachusetts—the center of the American Anti-Slavery Society—to Rochester, New York, where the American and Foreign Anti-Slavery Society, a competing group with different political philosophies, was headquartered. (One of the reasons the American and Foreign Anti-Slavery Society had split off from Garrison's group in 1840 was that its members believed violence was justified as a means to end slavery.) In Rochester, Douglass and black leaders Martin Delany and William Nell began publishing the *North Star.* The first issue came out on December 3, 1847, and Douglass would continue editing and publishing newspapers for more than 25 years. His papers included the *North Star*

In 1847, Douglass began to publish his own antislavery newspaper, the North Star, *which allowed him to express his own abolitionist views.*

(1847-1851), *Frederick Douglass' Paper* (1851-1860), *Douglass' Monthly* (1860-1867), and the *New National Era* (1870-1873).

In addition to his involvement in black antislavery activities, Douglass also pursued other reform efforts, including women's rights, temperance (opposition to the use of alcohol), and various educational and peace reforms. In an 1845 speech, he had argued that "all great reforms go together," and he had consistently compared the oppression of working people and the racist attitudes of northerners to the institution of slavery in the South. In 1848, Douglass participated in the historic convention at Seneca Falls, New York, that sparked the women's rights movement in the United States. He was the only man at the meeting to speak in support of women's suffrage. There he became friends with women's rights activists Elizabeth Cady Stanton and Susan B. Anthony, with whom he would work for decades.

Influenced by members of the American and Foreign Anti-Slavery Society—especially Gerrit Smith, who had provided generous funding for the *North Star*—Douglass began to seriously question some of Garrison's politics. He now viewed the U.S. Constitution as a document that could be used to combat slavery. He also came to believe that slavery should be abolished throughout the United States instead of splitting the country into two nations, slave and free. Finally, Douglass decided that "moral suasion" alone would not end slavery. Instead,

This 1850 daguerreotype shows Douglass (seated at left) at an antislavery meeting in Cazenovia, New York.

direct action—even the violence that the Garrisonians abhorred—would probably have to be employed.

In May 1851, Douglass publicly revealed his changed views at the American Anti-Slavery Society's annual meeting. From then on, his relationship with Garrison was strained, and it ended completely in 1853 when Garrison accused Douglass of having an affair with Julia Griffiths, a white British antislavery activist who worked with Douglass on his newspaper. Douglass's views also differed from those of many of his fellow black abolitionists, such as Martin Delany, who were calling for establishing colonies for black Americans in Africa.

In the late 1840s, Douglass had become friends with a white man named John Brown. Brown fought against slavery in Kansas in the mid-1850s and believed that God wanted him to free every slave. He developed a plan for a series of fortified Underground Railroad stations in the Appalachian Mountains. In 1859, Brown told Douglass of his plans to capture the federal arsenal at Harpers Ferry, Virginia, and give the guns stored there to slaves so they could fight for their freedom. Douglass tried without success to talk his friend out of this rash deed.

Brown's revolt failed, and he was hanged for treason on December 2, 1859. Because Douglass had known of Brown's plan, a warrant was issued for his arrest. After first fleeing to Canada, Douglass once again went to England. He had been there for only three months when he heard that Annie, his 10-year-old daughter, had died in March 1860. Douglass immediately returned home and was able to remain in the country because the government by then had decided not to prosecute any of the others who had been implicated in the John Brown conspiracy. He then began to publish *Douglass' Monthly* and resumed speaking engagements in August.

In 1860, the United States was in the middle of a fierce presidential campaign. Although Abraham Lincoln, who represented the antislavery Republican Party, did not plan to abolish slavery in the existing states, several southern states still threatened to secede from the Union if he were elected. After his election, first South Carolina, and then Mississippi, Florida, Alabama, Georgia, Louisiana, and Texas left the United States. On February 4, 1861, they formed the Confederate States of America. When the Confederates bombed Fort Sumter, South Carolina, on April 12, 1861, Congress declared war.

In speech after speech during the Civil War, Douglass called for the president to grant all slaves their freedom. On January 1, 1863, President Lincoln issued the Emancipation Proclamation, which freed all slaves in the Confederacy, although not those living in the loyal border states, where slavery remained legal.

Douglass's next battle was getting black soldiers into the Union army. In January 1863, he convinced President Lincoln to allow blacks to enlist. He then helped to recruit for the black 54th and 55th Massachusetts Regiments. Despite promises of equality, the Union army treated black soldiers unfairly. They were poorly trained and given low-level assignments, and their salaries were less than those of the white soldiers. They were also refused promotions to positions of leadership. Douglass

Frederick Douglass helped recruit soldiers for the 54th Massachusetts Regiment (here attacking Fort Wagner, South Carolina) and was proud that two of his own sons, Lewis and Charles, served with this famous unit.

again met with Lincoln, who promised to talk to the army about equal pay for black soldiers. The soldiers finally received larger paychecks in October 1864.

After the Civil War ended, Douglass lobbied extensively for the Freedmen's Bureau (which provided poor blacks with medical, educational, and financial assistance) and supported the establishment of the Freedmen's Bank. He also worked for the passage of several new amendments to the U.S. Constitution. The Thirteenth Amendment, which passed in 1865, abolished slavery throughout the United States. The Fourteenth Amendment (1868) guaranteed the rights of citizenship for all Americans, and the Fifteenth Amendment (1870) extended voting rights to black men.

To maintain his political influence, Douglass resettled in Washington, D.C. He was appointed head of the Freedmen's Bank in 1874. When the bank collapsed that same year (due to financial difficulties that had preceded Douglass's appointment), many blacks who lost their hard-earned savings blamed Douglass. Some black leaders were also suspicious of Douglass's lack of religious zeal and his strong commitment to the Republican Party.

When Reconstruction ended in 1877, Douglass viewed its failure as being primarily economic. Without land, jobs, and skills, former slaves had no way of attaining economic independence. At first, Douglass opposed black people migrating from the South, but he gradually came to realize that blacks would probably have to relocate in the North to experience true freedom and security.

In 1877, Douglass received the first of what would be several federal appointments when President Rutherford B. Hayes named him U.S. marshal of the District of Columbia. He served as Washington, D.C.'s recorder of deeds from 1881 to 1886. And from 1889 to 1891, Douglass represented the United States in Haiti.

Two years after Douglass's wife, Anna, died in 1882, Douglass remarried. His new wife, Helen Pitts, a white woman from an abolitionist family who was about 20 years younger than Douglass, worked in Douglass's recorder of deeds office.

When Frederick Douglass married Helen Pitts (1838-1903) in 1884—photographed on their Niagara Falls honeymoon—their interracial marriage caused a stir in the abolitionist community, and was opposed by Douglass's own children.

In the decades following the Civil War, Douglass continued fighting for black civil and economic rights as well as for other reform efforts. On February 20, 1895, he spoke at a women's rights meeting. Later that evening, at the age of 77, Douglass died of a heart attack.

Funeral services for Frederick Douglass were held in three different churches in Washington, D.C. Thousands of people, from schoolchildren to well-known politicians and activists, came to honor him. As they looked back on the life of Frederick Douglass, the mourners could see the transformation that he recounted in *Narrative of the Life of Frederick Douglass*: "How a slave was made a man."

Harriet Tubman (1820?-1913), who was called
"General Tubman" by militant abolitionist John Brown,
helped hundreds of slaves escape north to freedom.

6

Harriet Ross Tubman
Traveling Freedom's Road

*H*arriet Ross Tubman became known as the "Moses" of her people. Like the biblical Moses who led the Israelites out of slavery in Egypt, Tubman led blacks out of slavery in the American South. In the decade following her own escape in 1849, she would guide more than 300 slaves to freedom on the Underground Railroad. Later, during the Civil War, Tubman's bravery and her ability to move about unnoticed in forested areas made her valuable to the Union army. After the war, she spent the rest of her life fighting for various reforms, including women's rights and temperance.

91

Harriet Tubman was born in 1820 or 1821, one of 11 children. Her father, Benjamin Ross, was a free black, and her mother, Harriet Greene Ross, was a slave on the Joseph Brodess plantation on Maryland's Eastern Shore. Named Araminta, Harriet was called Minty until she was a teenager, when she took her mother's name.

When he married in 1824, Edward Brodess took over the estate from his father. He was not a skilled manager and, in order to generate more income, he began selling off many of his slaves, especially women in their childbearing years. Two of Harriet's older sisters were sold away from their family.

As soon as Harriet was old enough to work, her owner began to hire her out to other farmers in the area. Even as a child, Harriet had a mind of her own. As punishment for being defiant, she was often abused and treated poorly. Frequently, she would be sent back to the Brodess plantation ill with pneumonia and exhausted from overwork. At other times, she returned badly beaten. One of the women she worked for would whip her when she was not able to stay awake all night rocking an infant so it wouldn't cry. Harriet's loving mother would always nurse her difficult child back to health.

Harriet's inability to take orders worried her parents, who wanted her to be a house slave, not a field hand. But after she had worked indoors for seven years, Harriet's master hired her out as a field worker. While this made her mother sad, Harriet secretly felt as if she had won a victory because she believed no one would bother her in the fields if she did her work well.

During Harriet's childhood, tension over the issue of slavery was increasing. The failed uprising of Denmark Vesey in Charleston, South Carolina, in 1822 made both whites and blacks remember the 1800 insurrection plot of Gabriel in Richmond, Virginia, and especially the successful slave revolution in Haiti in the 1790s. In 1831, when Harriet was about 10 years old, Nat Turner's rebellion spread even more hysteria across the South.

The fear of slave revolts led to an increase in the number of white patrols, who terrorized blacks who were caught out at night without passes. White southerners also banned slave meetings, including religious gatherings, and prohibited teaching slaves to read or write (skills that Harriet never learned). What little freedom the slaves possessed had been stripped from them. Young Harriet often had nightmares about being sold away from her family or being tormented by the patrols.

It was because of these threats and restrictions that Harriet, like many slaves, grew up fearing whites and wanting freedom more than anything. As a child, she no doubt heard stories about people who would help slaves to flee to the North. The network that in the 1840s would become known as the Underground Railroad had been helping slaves escape ever since the late 1700s. The Underground Railroad was not a real railroad, but a secret network of men and women who risked their lives and freedom to help runaway slaves. Whites—often Quakers and Methodists who believed that slavery was wrong— and free blacks provided safe homes along the road to freedom. "Conductors" guided the runaway slaves from

Exact numbers are unknown, but it is estimated that several hundred slaves escaped on the Underground Railroad each year in the 30 years before the Civil War.

"station" to "station," where "stationmasters" hid the fugitives in houses, cellars, barns, and haystacks. With their help and guided by the North Star in the night sky, it was possible—even though very difficult—for slaves to escape north without being caught.

Although Harriet must also have known that many slaves and free blacks would help any fugitive who came along, she would not have an opportunity to run away for a long time. When she was 14 or 15, she suffered a severe head injury that would plague her for the rest of her life. An overseer accidentally hit Harriet in the head with a two-pound lead weight when she blocked his path as he chased a slave who was trying to escape a beating. The blow knocked Harriet unconscious and she would experience seizures and sleeping spells until her death.

During her slow recovery, Harriet became deeply religious and even prayed for her master's soul. When she heard, however, that Brodess was planning to sell her and her brothers south—away from the rest of their family and farther from the free states—Harriet prayed, "Lord, if you ain't never going to change that man's heart, kill him, Lord, and take him out of the way, so he won't do no more mischief." Throughout her life, Harriet continued to believe that God was on her side and would intercede against slaveholders and slave catchers.

When she recovered, Anthony "Doc" Thompson, who managed the plantation for Brodess, hired Harriet out again. Because she was such a good worker, he let her keep a small portion of her earnings. Harriet now worked for John Stewart, a shipbuilder and timber operator, who also employed Ben Ross, Harriet's father. Stewart trusted Ross and had made him a supervisor for one of his lumbering crews.

As father and daughter worked together, Ross began to teach Harriet skills such as how to pick a path through the woods without making a sound. She also learned how to find roots and herbs for curing various illnesses. Harriet knew that her father was teaching her what she needed to know in order to escape from slavery.

In 1844, Harriet Ross fell in love and married a free black man named John Tubman. To bring something of her own into the marriage, she made a beautiful quilt to decorate their new home. While Harriet became more discontented about being a slave, John was unconcerned about her not being free and laughed at her fears about being sold and her desire for freedom.

A year following her marriage, Harriet paid a lawyer $5 to look up the wills of all her mother's owners. She discovered that, according to one of the wills, her mother should have been freed years ago when she had reached the age of 45. This injustice drove Harriet to think even more about freedom, and she began to have visions and dreams that urged her to escape.

In 1849, Harriet learned that Doc Thompson was planning to sell her and three of her brothers south to Georgia, where escape to the North would be all but impossible. She decided that now was the time to run away, and she convinced her brothers to go with her.

The four started their long journey at night, Tubman leading her brothers through the woods. After a while, the three men announced that they were turning back. They feared the patrollers with their bloodhounds, getting whipped, and especially being sold farther south if they were caught. The four of them returned to the plantation, but Tubman escaped alone two days later. Recalling her decision, Tubman would later say:

> I had reasoned this out in my mind; there was one of two things I had a right to, liberty or death; if I could not have one, I would have the other; for no man should take me alive; I should fight for my liberty as long as my strength lasted, and when the time came for me to go, the Lord would let them take me.

Wanting someone to know that she was leaving, Tubman headed for the Big House to tell Mary Ann Bowley, who was her niece or half sister. But because Thompson was approaching, she walked back to the quarters singing a song:

When that old chariot comes,
I'm going to leave you.
I'm bound for the promised land.
Friends, I'm going to leave you.

Taking little more than her wedding quilt, Tubman left behind everything and everyone she knew. To protect herself and others, she never revealed who had helped her escape. Years later, a woman who had known Harriet Tubman claimed that Tubman had told her that she had been guided to the next stations on the Underground Railroad by a Quaker woman from a nearby town. In gratitude, Tubman had given the woman her patchwork quilt. She continued to be taken from one station to the next, often hiding for days in root cellars, until she finally reached freedom in Pennsylvania. (It is also possible that Tubman escaped on her own by using the survival lessons her father had taught her and following the North Star.)

Later in her life, Tubman told biographer Sarah Bradford that when she arrived in Pennsylvania, "There was such a glory over everything, the sun came like gold through the trees and over the fields, and I felt like I was in heaven." Not believing her good fortune, Tubman "looked at my hands to see if I was the same person now I was free." For the rest of the year, Tubman worked in Philadelphia as a cook and a maid, enjoying the freedom of being able to quit a job for any reason. But while Philadelphia had the largest black community of any city in the North at that time, Tubman still missed her family.

Early in 1850, Tubman went to the office of the Philadelphia Vigilance Committee, an organization that helped runaway slaves. There she discovered the extent of the Underground Railroad and learned that Philadelphia was its central point in the eastern states. William Still, a free black who was the committee's director, kept extensive records on the fugitives he helped so that he could pass along information and reunite families. Through his efforts, Tubman sometimes heard about her relatives back in Maryland.

The Philadelphia Vigilance Committee had been formed to counteract the Fugitive Slave Act of 1850, which the government hoped would prevent its citizens from helping slaves escape to the North. By law, sheriffs and other authorities could now confiscate the property and possessions of anyone who was caught helping slaves to escape. The Fugitive Slave Act of 1850 made the trip back to the South more dangerous for the "conductors" who led runaway slaves north to freedom and for the "stationmasters" who sheltered the fugitives because their activities now made them subject to the death penalty.

The law also made life in the North more insecure for both free blacks and fugitive slaves. Any black person accused by a white of being a runaway could be hauled before a commissioner, who would determine the black's legal status. Since the commissioner's fee for deciding that a black was a fugitive was twice the amount as that for

As this 1851 poster warns, the Fugitive Slave Act of 1850—seen by many as an example of the federal government bowing to southern demands—greatly intensified the risks for escaping slaves and those who helped them.

declaring the black free, even free blacks were not safe. Rumors abounded that free blacks were being kidnapped and sold into slavery at huge profits to the kidnappers.

Despite these new dangers, Tubman decided that "I was free, and [my family] should be free also. . . . I would bring them all here." After meeting her niece or half sister, Mary Ann Bowley, and Mary Ann's two children in Baltimore and guiding them to Philadelphia in December 1850, she began her decade of leading slaves to freedom. A second trip to Baltimore brought Tubman's brother John and two other slaves to freedom.

More than two years after she had left Maryland, Tubman returned to her old home, hoping to convince her husband to return with her to Philadelphia. But when she knocked on his cabin door, she discovered that he had remarried. She then willed herself to forget John Tubman forever. By late that night, Tubman had gathered a group of 10 slaves and headed for Philadelphia with them. As always, by following the North Star and relying on the Underground Railroad for shelter, Harriet safely got her small group of runaways north to freedom.

For the next few years, Tubman continued to make frequent trips into the South. Her expeditions were funded by William Still of the Philadelphia Vigilance Committee and Thomas Garrett, who were probably the two most important stationmasters on the Underground Railroad. As Tubman's legendary status grew, other anti-slavery activists also helped to finance her trips. Slaves and admirers began to call her "Moses" because she led slaves to the "Promised Land" of freedom.

Because the Fugitive Slave Act had left northern cities unsafe for slaves, Tubman, starting in December 1851, began leading the fugitives farther north into Canada. The longer trip was harder, and sometimes the travelers had to go for days without food. Because any person deciding to turn back would betray the entire group and cause the Underground Railroad stationmasters to face criminal prosecution, Tubman carried her shotgun, swearing to use it if everyone didn't keep going.

During the 1850s, as the United States moved closer to a civil war, Tubman made up to 19 trips into Maryland

Twice a year for a decade, Harriet Tubman (far left) led slaves, such as the seven shown here, to freedom. It was said that not one of the fugitives Tubman had helped was ever recaptured.

and led more than 300 slaves to freedom. She rescued her parents and all of her brothers and sisters, except for one sister who had died before Tubman could return for her. As Harriet Tubman became a legend among both slaves and southern whites, slaves began to believe that she could never be caught. They said she could see in the dark like an owl and smell danger down wind like a deer. They claimed she could move through thick brush without making a sound and was so strong that she could carry a grown man. Slaveholders wanted her stopped and offered rewards totaling $40,000 for her capture.

In 1858, Tubman met John Brown, a white man who planned to set up armed forts in the Appalachian Mountains to help slaves escape. He asked Tubman to tell him everything she knew about the Underground Railroad and was so impressed with her that he called her "General Tubman." A year later, when Brown decided to organize a revolution against slavery by seizing the government's store of arms at Harpers Ferry, Virginia, Tubman enthusiastically supported his plan—a plan that Frederick Douglass found too extreme. When Brown's attack on Harpers Ferry failed, and the U.S. government captured and hanged him, Tubman grieved deeply for the man she called the "Savior of our People."

When the Civil War broke out in 1861, Tubman welcomed a new opportunity to fight slavery. She worked for the Union army—first as a cook and a nurse and later as a scout and a spy. In May 1862, the Union army sent Tubman to Beaufort, one of the islands off the coast of South Carolina. There she provided aid to slaves who had

Harriet Tubman was never paid for her services to the Union army, which included recruiting soldiers, scouting and spying, and domestic labor.

been left on the island following the Union army's victory over Confederate forces. Tubman taught them skills to support themselves and encouraged them to volunteer for the Union army. When Lincoln allowed blacks to become soldiers in January 1863, Tubman began working as a nurse, using her knowledge of herbs and roots to make medications for the soldiers who were hospitalized.

Later in the war, Tubman became a Union spy, gathering information by using her expertise at disguises and her ability to move around without being noticed. She led teams of black scouts behind enemy lines and also marched with the Union troops when they raided the

South. In the successful Combahee River raid in South Carolina, her troops destroyed Confederate armaments that she and her scouts had located. She also continued to recruit former slaves for the Union army.

Over the years, Tubman would become close associates with many antislavery activists and reformers, including Thomas Garrett, Susan B. Anthony, and William Still. In 1857, several abolitionist friends in Auburn, New York, had helped Tubman buy a house for her parents.

After the Civil War ended in 1865, Tubman returned to Auburn to care for her aging parents. She raised funds for schools for black children and collected clothes for the poor. In 1869, she married Nelson Davis,

Secretary of State William H. Seward (1801-1872) was an outspoken opponent of slavery in the Lincoln administration. A friend of Tubman's, Seward sold her a house for her parents.

a black veteran. (John Tubman had been murdered by a white southerner in 1867.) Sarah Bradford, a white schoolteacher in Auburn, conducted extensive interviews with Tubman for her 1868 biography, *Scenes in the Life of Harriet Tubman*. Proceeds from the sales of that book and Bradford's revised and expanded edition, *Harriet Tubman: The Moses of Her People*, helped Tubman to pay for her parents' home and provided some funding for her charity work.

In the years following the war, Tubman made numerous speeches for women's rights and temperance. She was a delegate to the 1896 convention of the National Federation of Afro-American Women, a group founded by Booker T. Washington's wife, Margaret Murray Washington. Her religious fervor remained strong, and she was active in promoting the growth of the African Methodist Episcopal Zion Church in upstate New York.

Tubman spent the last few years of her life at the Harriet Tubman Home for Aged and Indigent Colored People in Auburn—which she had helped to found in 1903. When she died of pneumonia on March 10, 1913, local Civil War veterans fired a cannon in her honor at her funeral. A year later, Booker T. Washington was the featured speaker at the unveiling of a plaque in Auburn that commemorated her heroism. In 1978, the United States Postal Service released a 13-cent stamp bearing her image. All of these acts were fitting tributes to the courageous woman who had fought so untiringly not only for her own freedom but also for the freedom and dignity of all black people in the United States.

The most powerful black man in the United States from 1895 until his death, Booker T. Washington (1856-1915) founded a school for black students where they learned the practical skills he felt were needed to lift them out of poverty.

7

Booker T. Washington
From Slave to Educator

*B*ooker Taliaferro Washington was the most influential black leader of his time, and he wielded a considerable amount of power among both blacks and whites. He advised U.S. presidents on race relations and helped to decide political appointments for blacks throughout the nation. In addition, he determined which black-owned businesses should receive financial support, and he also exerted a great deal of control over the newspapers and magazines that were written and published by blacks.

Many of Washington's actions and opinions were controversial. He argued that learning a trade was more important than gaining political power or equality by integrating schools, neighborhoods, and public places. Instead of fighting discrimination and segregation, Washington believed that black people should concentrate on improving themselves through industrial education.

Booker T. Washington was born in 1856, the son of an unknown white man and Jane, a slave cook who was owned by James Burroughs of Franklin County, Virginia. Booker and his mother lived in a one-room log cabin that also served as the kitchen on the Burroughs plantation. They had no furniture and slept on ragged blankets on the dirt floor. Jane cooked the meals for the master's family and the other slaves in their large fireplace.

Booker's mother married a slave named Washington Ferguson after his birth. When the Civil War ended in 1865, nine-year-old Booker and his family, now free, left Virginia and traveled by foot over the mountains to Malden, West Virginia, where Ferguson found work in the salt mines. Although the family was still poor, they were no longer slaves.

Booker's first job was packing salt into barrels at the salt mine where his stepfather worked; he also worked in the coal mines. Because the black miners wanted a better future for their children, they decided that a school was needed. When an educated black man from Ohio arrived in Malden, they enlisted him to teach their children. Booker desperately wanted to attend classes, but his stepfather told him that the family needed what little money he was able to earn. Booker continued to plead to be allowed to go to school, and his parents finally relented.

After the Civil War, menial, low-wage, and often dangerous jobs were all that was available to free but uneducated blacks, such as those working in this phosphate mine.

When the teacher first asked Booker to state his full name, he blurted out, "Booker Washington." From then on, his stepfather's first name was Booker's surname.

Booker Washington would spend his days in the salt mine and then attend school at night. Eventually, his stepfather allowed him to enroll in day classes if he continued to work seven hours every day in the mine. So Booker was in the mine from 4 A.M. to 9 A.M. before classes started and for two more hours after school.

When Booker was 14 or 15 years old, he learned that General Ruffner, who owned the salt mine, needed someone to help around his house. Despite rumors that Ruffner's wife was so strict that their workers seldom lasted more than several weeks, Booker applied for and got the job. Although he was once so discouraged that he ran away, Washington later credited Viola Ruffner with teaching him to be neat, prompt, and honest. Booker became close to Mrs. Ruffner, who even gave the young man extra school lessons.

It was in 1872 that Booker heard about an industrial trade school for blacks in Virginia. At Hampton Normal and Agricultural Institute, "poor but worthy students" could work to earn their board and gain an education. Carrying a worn suitcase, 16-year-old Booker set out for Hampton with only a few dollars in his pocket.

Washington made the 500-mile trip by stagecoach to the school in the state where he had been born a slave. When he ran out of money for the stagecoach, he walked the dusty, rutted roads or hitched rides on wagons. He earned some extra money by doing odd jobs along the way, but many nights he would sleep under wooden sidewalks, using his suitcase for a pillow.

When Washington finally arrived at Hampton, he was hungry, tired, and dirty. The head teacher frowned at his crumpled clothing and tattered appearance. But instead of sending him away, she put him to work cleaning the classroom. Knowing that this was the teacher's way of testing his industriousness, Washington promptly did the work and passed her exam with flying colors.

Within a few days, the school's principal, Samuel Chapman Armstrong, found someone to sponsor Washington and pay his tuition. To earn his room and board, Washington worked as a janitor at the school.

110

In his autobiography, *Up from Slavery*, Washington recalled that among the first lessons he learned at Hampton Normal and Agricultural Institute were how to sleep in a bed with sheets, use a toothbrush, and how to eat at a table with a knife, fork, and spoon, and a napkin. All of this was new to the former slave and miner.

Hampton Institute strived to develop its black students into model citizens with the skills they needed for success. During his three years at Hampton, Washington studied geography, grammar, history, and science, and he

Booker T. Washington got his first taste of industrial education at the Hampton Institute, where he met his mentor, General Samuel Chapman Armstrong.

also learned various handicrafts and farming skills. One of his teachers tutored him in public speaking, and he became the leader of the debate team. His powerful oratory would later make him one of the most famous speakers of the nineteenth and early twentieth centuries.

In 1875, Washington graduated from Hampton Institute with honors. After teaching at the school for black children in his hometown of Malden for three years, Washington enrolled at the Wayland Seminary in Washington, D.C. Unlike Hampton's course of study, Wayland's curriculum was entirely academic. After a year at Wayland, Washington decided that learning practical skills was far better than learning only philosophies and theories. Dissatisfied, Booker T. Washington left the seminary and the big city life of Washington, D.C.

In 1879, at the invitation of General Armstrong, he returned to Hampton Institute to address the graduating class. Several weeks later, Armstrong offered Washington a teaching position at a monthly wage of $25. While teaching at Hampton, Washington supervised the training of 75 American Indians who were students there.

Washington's big break came the following year when Colonel Wilbur F. Foster, a former Confederate officer, and Arthur L. Brooks were running for the Alabama state legislature. To win the election, they needed the support of Macon County's black voters. Lewis Adams, a former slave and a leader in the black community, told Foster and Brooks that in order to get the black vote, they would have to promise to provide the funds to establish a school for blacks following the

112

election. In exchange for their pledge, Adams encouraged the black people in Macon County to vote for Foster and Brooks. Soon after their victory, the Alabama legislature appropriated funds "to establish a Normal School for colored teachers at Tuskegee."

A board composed of three commissioners was established to get the school off the ground. When they asked the principal of Hampton Institute to recommend someone for the position of principal at the Tuskegee Normal and Industrial Institute, General Armstrong proposed that they hire Washington. Washington accepted their offer.

When he arrived in Tuskegee, Washington was dismayed to find that the school did not yet exist. There was no land or buildings and no books or teachers. The Alabama legislature had set aside $2,000 for starting the school, but the money would not be available until the following year.

Beginning with nothing, Washington managed to build a school. He traveled throughout the surrounding rural area, meeting poor black farmers, and he spoke in Tuskegee's black churches. He told everyone about the school he was starting in Tuskegee and invited young black men and women to apply for admission. Thirty students were selected for Tuskegee's first class.

Washington began classes on July 4, 1881— Independence Day. Tuskegee's original site was the local African Methodist Episcopal church, a building in such poor condition that when it rained, water poured in through holes in the roof.

In order to purchase a better facility, Washington borrowed $200 from General James Marshall, the treasurer at Hampton Institute. With this money, he made a down payment on a local farm where slaves had once lived while toiling for their owner. Blacks and whites from the community volunteered tools, labor, and additional money. With the help of his students, Washington cleared over 20 acres of woodland, providing lumber for building and fields for growing crops. As the students worked, they learned the value of manual labor. They erected most of the school's buildings and grew much of their own food. Then they built a kiln for making the bricks that were used for the buildings.

Although Tuskegee had been intended to be a school for teachers, when Washington had seen the living conditions of the rural blacks, he decided that domestic and agricultural skills and manual trades—even basic living skills—were more immediate needs. So, at the school, young men learned carpentry, masonry, and farming, and young women learned homemaking skills. Washington also taught his students the basics of personal hygiene and stressed the importance of good manners and honesty.

Tuskegee's student body grew quickly, tripling in the first few months. Washington hired additional teachers, many of whom were Hampton graduates. Olivia A. Davidson, the newly hired assistant principal, had a genius for fundraising. During the 1880s, she and Washington made many highly successful tours throughout the North to raise money for the school. Benefit suppers and literary readings organized by students and teachers also

To many young blacks, Tuskegee Institute (now Tuskegee University), stood as a symbol of the success and prosperity that they could achieve in the United States.

amassed needed funds for salaries and facilities. With a larger staff, Tuskegee could both educate teachers and train workers for manual occupations.

While Tuskegee was flourishing, Washington's personal life during this time was often filled with tragedy. In 1882, he had married Fannie N. Smith, and their daughter, Portia Marshall Washington, was born in 1883. Fannie died in the following year at the age of 26. In 1885, Washington married Olivia A. Davidson, Tuskegee's valuable assistant principal. Unfortunately, Olivia also

115

died young, only a few months after the birth of their second child. Washington married for a third time in 1892, and Margaret Murray Washington would be his wife until he died. Margaret Washington, the new assistant principal, also directed all of the girls' courses at the school and began programs for local women as well.

By this time, the Tuskegee Normal and Industrial Institute was making a name for itself. The school's good reputation was spread partly by its graduates, who went out into the community to teach people the skills they had learned at Tuskegee. In 1892, the first annual Tuskegee Negro Conference was held for the purpose of discussing the progress of black people. Although Washington had invited fewer than 100 black people to the conference, more than 500 attended.

For its faculty, Tuskegee had attracted some of the most talented blacks in the country. One such individual was agricultural chemist George Washington Carver, who came to Tuskegee in 1896 to teach agriculture and run the school's experiment station. Always seeking to improve the lives of southern black farmers, Carver promoted crop diversification—the practice of planting a variety of crops to guard against diseases and soil erosion—and other measures that would improve the soil. His experiments at Tuskegee on new uses for a variety of plants, especially the peanut, benefited many and won him lasting fame.

Washington's reputation had spread along with Tuskegee's. He had become an effective educator and, with the death of Frederick Douglass in 1895, became a spokesman for many blacks. Between 1865 and 1895,

As the director of agricultural research at Tuskegee Institute from 1896 until his death, George Washington Carver (1864?-1943) greatly improved the economy of the South with his many innovations, including developing hundreds of uses for the peanut.

ex-slaves had become more educated. Black colleges and institutes blossomed, and white colleges had begun admitting black students. Blacks were now full citizens. They could vote, serve on juries, and send representatives to the U.S. Congress. They were also becoming judges, lieutenant governors, and school superintendents.

Black people's political gains, however, had gradually eroded in the years since federal troops had been withdrawn from the South in 1877. Southern legislatures had passed "Jim Crow" laws that enforced segregated facilities in public places and on public transportation, and blacks had been left in poorly funded schools that were inferior to those for whites. Lynchings of blacks also were on the rise. This change in the racial climate alarmed Washington. Worried about losing funding for his school, he decided that he must try to placate white people's hatred and fears as best he could.

In 1895, Washington was invited to speak to a large audience in Atlanta, Georgia, at the Cotton States and International Exposition. It was here that his message of bettering oneself through industrial education and hard work reached a nationwide audience. In his speech, Washington described the state of former slaves and provided a vision of their future:

> Ignorant and inexperienced, it is not strange that in the first years of our new life we began at the top instead of at the bottom; that a seat in Congress or the State Legislature was more sought than real estate or industrial skill; that the political convention or stump speaking had more attractions than starting a dairy farm or truck garden. . . . No race can prosper till it learns that there is as much dignity in tilling a field as in writing a poem. It is at the bottom of life we must begin, and not at the top.

Washington also told the multiracial audience that he believed black people were wasting their time in the "agitation of questions of social equality." Instead, he

Booker T. Washington's powerful oratory won him the admiration of many Americans—both black and white—while attracting criticism from others, especially blacks who felt that Washington failed to confront white racism.

maintained that the "enjoyment of all the privileges that will come . . . must be the result of severe and constant struggle rather than of artificial forcing." Southern whites should be seen not as enemies but as partners in the economic growth of black Americans. Appealing to those whites who supported segregation, Washington argued that blacks and whites could remain "separate as the fingers" while working together "as the hand."

Clapping wildly, the white people in the audience raved over his speech, tossing their canes and hats into the air. The reaction of blacks to the speech was varied. Former abolitionist William Still reported that blacks in the audience had cried tears of joy because Washington had given them hope for a more secure future. Other blacks felt he had been too ready to exchange civil rights for economic gains. The Atlanta *Advocate*, a newspaper published by blacks, called him "Professor Bad Taste" for trying so hard to please whites.

Following the speech—which became known by its black critics as the "Atlanta Compromise"—Washington's political power among white people increased. He continued to voice his belief that through hard work, blacks could eventually advance and gain equality. While southern blacks would still be second-class citizens, he insisted that they would share in some of the benefits of southern prosperity because relations between the races would be improved.

White people throughout the country invited Washington to speak about race relations for fees of thousands of dollars for each appearance, and magazine editors asked him to write articles. He received an honorary degree from Harvard University. The publication of Washington's autobiography, *Up from Slavery*, in 1901, brought him even more fame.

With his newly acquired power and recognition, Washington began building the "Tuskegee Machine," a network of black institutions that he controlled either directly or indirectly. The Tuskegee Machine exerted influence that amounted to censorship over a large percentage of newspapers and magazines that were published by blacks. In addition, through his National Negro Business League, he could decide which black-owned businesses to help financially.

Washington also had tremendous political influence. His political power grew even stronger in 1901 when Vice-President Theodore Roosevelt became president after William McKinley was assassinated. Washington became a close political advisor to the new president, who during eight years in office rarely appointed a black to any political post without first consulting Washington.

By the early 1900s, W. E. B. Du Bois, who would help to found the National Association for the Advancement of Colored People in 1910, and other important black leaders were openly criticizing Booker T. Washington. Washington did not welcome Du Bois's outspoken criticism. But Du Bois, a history professor with a Ph.D. from Harvard and author of the now-classic *The Souls of Black Folks*, pointed out that Washington's Atlanta Compromise had only hurt his people. Because of restrictions against blacks, especially in the South, they

W. E. B. Du Bois (1868-1963) was Booker T. Washington's most outspoken critic. As a founder of the National Association for the Advancement of Colored People, he was also a threat to Washington's power.

were not getting the factory jobs for which Tuskegee had trained them. And their agricultural skills had not made it possible for them to purchase farm land. Du Bois and many other black leaders believed that, instead of simply learning how to work with their hands—performing many of the tasks they had done while they were slaves—their people should strive to get a college education.

Although Washington often appeared to appease white people, he had secretly funded two court tests of discriminatory laws during the early years of Theodore Roosevelt's presidency. These cases, *Giles v. Harris* (1903) and *Giles v. Teasley* (1904), attacked the voting restrictions that southern states had passed at the turn of the century. These laws prevented blacks from participating in elections by effectively limiting voters to only those whose ancestors had been registered voters before the end of the Civil War. Both cases went to the U.S. Supreme Court, where they were rejected on technicalities.

Still enmeshed in heated debate with Du Bois and other black leaders, Washington died from arteriosclerosis, a heart disease, on November 14, 1915, at the age of 59. He had taken ill in New York City but still managed to make his way back to Tuskegee before he died.

Today, Washington's legacy is mixed. Some people respect him for his tremendous power and influence in both black and white communities. They say that during his lifetime, he provided inspiration and leadership for future generations of black people and that he was correct in believing that blacks should focus on economic independence before demanding social equality. Other people remember Washington as a black man who accommodated whites by telling black people to avoid political action and to remain silent when they were faced with situations of discrimination and violent repression.

Whatever others thought of him, throughout his career as an educator and a political leader, Booker T. Washington steadfastly held to the advice he had given blacks in his controversial Atlanta Exposition speech:

> Cast down your bucket where you are; cast it down in making friends, in every manly way, of the people of all races by whom we are surrounded.

Born to newly freed slaves, Mary Church Terrell (1863-1954) engaged in a lifelong struggle for equal rights for blacks and women.

8

Mary Church Terrell
Lifting as She Climbed

*I*n a long life—beginning in the year of the Emancipation Proclamation and ending the year the U.S. Supreme Court ruled against school segregation—Mary Church Terrell worked to make life socially, politically, and economically better for black people and for women. In her fight for equality, she became one of the most respected civil rights leaders of her time.

Terrell was a founder of the National Association for the Advancement of Colored People (NAACP), an internationally known lecturer, a widely published writer, and a member of many boards and organizations. She also worked for the right of women to vote and hold political office. In 1953, at age 89, Terrell was still leading demonstrations in Washington, D.C.

On September 23, 1863, Mary Eliza Church was born in Memphis, Tennessee, the oldest child of Louisa Ayers Church and Robert Reed Church, who were both former slaves. Robert Church was the son of his master, Charles B. Church, and a slave woman named Emmeline. Robert's father treated him well, but he never gave him his freedom. When Robert was older, he worked on one of his father's Mississippi riverboats.

When the Union army took control of the Mississippi River, bringing an end to the riverboat trade, Robert Church settled in Memphis, which was then in Union hands. There he opened a saloon and courted Louisa Ayers, a house slave. The two were married while the Civil War raged, and, not long afterwards, the Emancipation Proclamation freed the couple. Both were shrewd businesspeople who were well established when Mary was born later that year. Louisa ran a successful hair salon, which served many of the wealthiest women in Memphis. Robert's saloon was also doing well, and the family was able to live comfortably. Louisa's business still made it possible for her to provide a good home for Mary and her younger child, Thomas, following her divorce when Mary was still very young. Robert continued to support his children and remained involved in their lives.

Even at a young age, Mary was aware that, compared to most black children, she had a privileged life. She began her education at a school for black children in

The elegant childhood home of Mary Church Terrell in Memphis reflected her family's wealth.

Memphis, but because it was so inferior, her parents decided to send her to Yellow Springs, Ohio, when she was seven. There she attended a boarding school that was operated by Antioch College and was frequently the only black child in her class. While she rarely had any problems with her classmates, one of them often called her racist names. In reaction, Mary was determined to show everyone that she was an outstanding student. She concentrated on her studies and soon stood at the head of her class academically. After two years at Antioch, Mary enrolled at a public school in Yellow Springs. After she finished the eighth grade, she went to a public high school in nearby Oberlin, Ohio, and graduated in 1879.

That same year brought a yellow fever epidemic to Memphis, causing many people to leave the city. Because they wanted to sell their houses quickly, Robert Church was able to buy a great deal of real estate at very cheap prices. Soon he was the South's first black millionaire. His wealth made him a part of the group of newly rich blacks, and the black politicians and educators whom he entertained would become role models for his daughter.

Mary's excellent academic record and her parents' financial status made it possible for her to attend Oberlin College, which had been founded in 1833 by a group of abolitionists. Oberlin had been admitting blacks since 1835, and it was one of the few integrated institutions of higher learning in the United States at that time.

Most women who attended Oberlin took a two-year program called the "ladies' course." But Mary Church instead chose the four-year "gentlemen's course." In addition to her classwork, Mary participated in a Bible study group, the campus church choir, and a literary society. She was also an editor of the school newspaper, the *Oberlin Review*. Mary was one of three black women to earn a bachelor's degree from Oberlin in 1884.

After her graduation, Mary returned to Memphis to live with her father. There she was expected to live the life of an educated and refined lady, attending teas and other social functions. In her father's home, Mary had the opportunity to associate with many nationally prominent blacks of the day. Former Mississippi senator Blanche Kelso Bruce and his wife were frequent visitors, and she became friends with Booker T. Washington, who often stopped by during his trips to raise money for the Tuskegee Normal and Industrial Institute. Mary was especially close to Frederick Douglass, probably the most celebrated black man of the time. She had first met him in 1881 at President James A. Garfield's inauguration, and their friendship would last until Douglass's death.

Through her family's connections, Mary Church Terrell met many influential black leaders of the day, including Frederick Douglass.

For a time, Mary was satisfied to be her father's hostess. But she soon longed to use her education to help others. When her father married Anna Wright shortly after Mary moved back to Memphis, Mary began to seek out a teaching position without telling her father.

In 1885, Mary Church was offered a job at Wilberforce, a black college in Wilberforce, Ohio, that had been founded by the African Methodist Episcopal Church before the Civil War. She taught there for two years before moving to Washington, D.C., to teach Latin at the M Street High School, a well-known public school for blacks. While teaching there full time, Church also completed the requirements for a master of arts degree in education from Oberlin College. In 1929, she would be named one of Oberlin's 100 most successful graduates during the college's first 94 years.

After Church began teaching, her father refused to speak to her for a year. Later, however, he was so proud of his daughter's accomplishments that he sent her on a tour of Europe. From 1888 to 1890, Church traveled and studied in Germany, France, Switzerland, Italy, and England. While living abroad, she had opportunities that black people in the United States never had, even if they were rich. In Europe, she could attend plays and concerts without encountering segregation or discrimination. Church enjoyed her new freedom and sense of equality. She even had several marriage proposals from European men (which she turned down). She considered staying in Europe, but she felt a need to return home and help blacks who were not as privileged as she was.

After returning to the United States in 1890, Church taught for one more year at the M Street School. Then she resigned to marry Robert Herberton Terrell, a black Harvard graduate who had been her department head at the school. (At the time, most U.S. school districts did not allow married women to teach.) In 1895, she was the first black woman to be appointed to the city's board of education, on which she served until 1901 and again from 1906 to 1911.

After her resignation, Mary Church Terrell devoted herself to public speaking, women's rights and civil rights, community organizing, and the black women's club movement. This network of local and regional groups under the direction of a national black women's organization was dedicated to uplifting black women through morality, education, and economic self-sufficiency. Because they were independent from both white women's and black men's organizations, these groups provided for middle-class black women an important opportunity to develop leadership skills and to address concerns that were unique to black women. By the 1910s, there would be 1,000 black women's clubs throughout the United States with a combined membership of 50,000.

In 1892, Terrell helped to organize the Colored Women's League. Made up mostly of teachers in the Washington, D.C., area, this organization ran a day care for children and evening classes for adults. The Colored Women's League joined with the National Federation of Afro-American Women in 1896 to form the National Association of Colored Women (NACW), which became the central organization of the black women's club movement. The NACW's motto was "Lifting As We Climb." The women created mothers' clubs as well as nurseries, orphanages, and kindergartens in an effort to help lift black women out of poverty. Terrell was the group's first president and later was named as its honorary president for life.

Although she was involved with work she enjoyed and found to be fulfilling, these early years of her marriage would be difficult ones for Terrell. Following three miscarriages—which she believed could have been avoided had Washington's segregated hospitals offered adequate health care for black women—she often suffered from depression. Hoping to find a better medical system, Terrell spent her fourth pregnancy in New York City, living with her mother. There, in 1898, she finally gave birth to a healthy daughter. Terrell named her Phyllis, after Phillis Wheatley, an eighteenth-century African American poet. (In 1905, Mary and Robert Terrell gave seven-year-old Phyllis a sister when they adopted Mary, the daughter of Mary Terrell's brother.)

Terrell's work for black women remained just as important following the birth of her daughter. When the black women's club movement began, there were two opposing schools of thought regarding black progress and equality. Booker T. Washington believed that blacks could achieve success and respect through hard work and self-sufficiency. At his school in Tuskegee, Alabama, Washington taught his black students industrial trades and agriculture as well as basic living skills.

Rather than focus on the industrial trades, W. E. B. Du Bois encouraged the "talented tenth" of the black population—those who held the most promise for the future—to pursue higher learning. He thought that black college graduates could become the intellectual and cultural leaders of their people. Unlike Washington, Du Bois advocated a constant struggle against racism and segregation.

Terrell was torn between these two views. At one point, she had worked with Booker T. Washington to keep Du Bois from becoming the assistant superintendent of schools in Washington, D.C. Still, she was critical of Washington's policy of accommodating whites, declaring that he compromised black people by not seeking an end to discrimination.

In 1909, at Du Bois's invitation, Terrell became a member of the Niagara Movement, a committee that had first met in 1905 and would organize as the National Association for the Advancement of Colored People (NAACP) in 1910. As Terrell and Du Bois worked together, their views became closer. Terrell served on the NAACP's first executive committee and became the vice-president of the District of Columbia branch that she had helped to organize.

Terrell was also active in women's organizations whose members were mostly white women. Although she never joined the National American Women's Suffrage Association (NAWSA) because the group's membership included so many southern white women, Terrell spoke for the group on many occasions. With NAWSA

As a charter member of the National Association for the Advancement of Colored People (NAACP), Mary Church Terrell helped to establish an organization that would fight lynching in the South and later play a significant role in the civil rights movement of the 1960s.

members, Terrell campaigned for the right of women to vote and worked with such famous suffragists as Susan B. Anthony and Carrie Chapman Catt. She also spoke to this group about the concerns of black women, who faced racism as well as sexism.

After women had won the right to vote in 1920, Terrell became active in the Republican Party. In the 1920s and 1930s, she organized black women to campaign for Republican candidates and was invited to Illinois to work on Ruth Hanna McCormick's Senate race in 1929. Three years later, Terrell served as an advisor to the Republican National Committee during President Herbert Hoover's reelection campaign.

Mary Church Terrell also represented U.S. women at international forums. She was in the U.S. delegation at the 1904 International Congress of Women in Berlin, Germany, where she impressed the audience with her flawless French and German. In 1919, she addressed the second congress of the Women's International League for Peace and Freedom (WILPF) in Zurich, Switzerland.

Terrell published her autobiography, *A Colored Woman in a White World*, in 1940. In that volume, she told her story of growing up black in a segregated white society. Even in her old age, she still faced the problem of segregation. In 1950, when she was 86, she protested against an illegal Jim Crow law that prohibited black people from eating in restaurants where white people ate, joining a small demonstration at Thompson's Restaurant in Washington, D.C. When the restaurant manager refused to serve the black patrons, the local activists sued the restaurant. The case went all the way to the U.S. Supreme Court, where Terrell testified. In 1953, the group of protesters won the case because segregation had been illegal in Washington, D.C., for 75 years. The group's actions helped to desegregate the nation's capital.

One of Terrell's last causes was fought for a woman named Rosa Ingram, who was a black sharecropper from Georgia. Along with her two sons, Ingram had been sentenced to death for killing a white man who had attacked them. Terrell led a delegation to the United Nations on their behalf. Due in part to her efforts, the state of Georgia finally freed the Ingrams in 1959.

Mary Church Terrell died on July 24, 1954, at the age of 90, two months after the Supreme Court had passed down its decision in the *Brown v. Board of Education of Topeka* case. The ruling was the long-awaited first blow against legal segregation in U.S. public schools.

Like many of the other black activists in this book, Terrell's battles were fought mostly on the written page, at the podium, or in the streets. Rather than using violent means, these leaders were untiring in their efforts to persuade their fellow white citizens to grant them freedom and equality. Famous for her eloquent speeches, Terrell's words remain an inspiration not only for black women, but for every U.S. citizen:

> We believe we can build the foundation of the next generation upon such a rock of morality, intelligence, and strength, that the floods of proscription, prejudice, and persecution may descend upon it in torrents and yet it will not be moved.

Serving as chairwoman of the Coordinating Committee for the Enforcement of the District of Columbia Anti-Discrimination Laws, Mary Church Terrell (shown here in her eighties) continued to fight for the rights of blacks, even taking to the streets to picket segregated stores in Washington, D.C.

Many black men and women—including those shown here—distinguished themselves in their fight to abolish slavery, establish religious and political rights for blacks, and improve the status of their race.

9

More Black Activists of the Nineteenth Century

*T*he leaders who have been profiled in this book are some of the best-known and most well respected nineteenth-century black activists, but there are many more. The following men and women represent the wide variety of views and the impressive array of accomplishments of other African Americans in the years before and after the Civil War. Many of them worked alongside the leaders in this book; others pursued their goals with people less remembered by history. All of them listened to the call of their conscience and devoted their lives to improving the status of black people in their time.

David **Walker** (1795?-1830) was born free in North Carolina and traveled widely before settling in Boston as a used clothing dealer. Entirely self-educated, he was a militant who believed in the right of blacks to rebel against slavery. In 1826, Walker helped found the General Coloured Association of Massachusetts, and he frequently wrote for *Freedom's Journal*, the first black newspaper. In his articles, he likened the suffering of black Americans to that of Jesus Christ.

Walker's lengthy tract, *David Walker's Appeal* (1829), called for violent rebellion against white masters, declaring that blacks deserved to enjoy the liberties of the free nation they had helped to build. Whites reacted with laws that prohibited both the distribution of the tract and slave literacy. The reward offered for Walker's capture may have led to his mysterious death in 1830. His *Appeal* survived, however, and led many later black abolitionists, including Henry Highland Garnet (and also some whites), to believe that violence against slavery was justified.

Born free in the North, **Maria Stewart** (1803-1879) was the first American woman to give speeches in public. Some of her lectures in Boston during 1832 and 1833 were later printed in the *Liberator*. Inspired by her devout Christianity, Stewart insisted that blacks had the same rights to liberty and equality as the American colonists who had won their independence from Great Britain in 1776. She rejected the plans of the mostly white American Colonization Society to send free blacks to Liberia, claiming that blacks had a right to freedom in the United States. After her brief speaking career—cut short because people believed that women should not speak in public—Stewart founded a school and a Sunday school and spent the rest of her life as a teacher.

Tunis Campbell (1812-1891) was born free in New Jersey and educated in boarding schools. He became a speaker for the antislavery movement, actively opposed the work of the American Colonization Society, and was a leader in the national black convention movement during the decades before the Civil War. During the Civil War, Campbell worked with the Department of War to resettle freed blacks in South Carolina. After the war, he became a superintendent for the Freedmen's Bureau on the sea islands off the Georgia coast. There he settled freed blacks on small independent farms that had formerly been plantations and established schools for their children.

In 1866, after the white head of the Freedmen's Bureau in Georgia banned him from the islands, Campbell bought an old plantation on the mainland and turned it into a communal farm for people from the islands. He was elected a state legislator in 1870 but lost his bid for reelection in 1872. He then served as justice of the peace until whites arrested him on a trumped-up charge and, in 1876, sentenced him to a year of hard labor. By the time of his release, the withdrawal of federal troops had left southern blacks defenseless, and Campbell was forced to spend the rest of his life in the North.

Alexander Crummell (1819-1898) was an Episcopalian minister who sought intellectual and social equality for blacks. In the 1830s and 1840s, he was active in the black convention and antislavery movements in

New York. A childhood neighbor and classmate of Henry Highland Garnet, Crummell earned a bachelor's degree from England's prestigious Cambridge University in 1853. He then went to Liberia as a missionary, believing that Christian, educated, and industrious American blacks had a responsibility to bring Western culture and religion to the Africans.

Crummell's promotion of black emigration to Liberia put him at odds with most of the black leaders of the day, however, for they believed the American Colonization Society sought to rid the U.S. of free blacks. After fleeing Liberia in the midst of a civil war in 1873, Crummell made his Washington, D.C., church a social center for blacks and, in 1897, helped to found the American Negro Academy, which encouraged the best-educated blacks to become leaders of their people.

William Still (1821-1902) was the executive secretary of Philadelphia's Anti-Slavery Society and was a major link in the Underground Railroad. Still published records in his volume, *The Underground Rail Road*, of his role in assisting runaway slaves, including Harriet Tubman. A staunch advocate of education as the key to black emancipation, Still said, "One thing is certain . . . our own education and elevation is to be one of the main levers to overthrow the institution of slavery in the United States."

As chairman of Philadelphia's Social, Civil, and Statistical Association, Still fought against the belief that former slaves were inferior to whites. He also served as the first president of a bank that helped blacks to purchase homes through low interest rates.

As director of the Philadelphia Vigilance Committee, William Still was one of the most successful "stationmasters" on the Underground Railroad.

Born free in Wilmington, Delaware, **Mary Ann Shadd Cary** (1823-1893) founded a school for blacks in her hometown in 1839 and taught for a decade. Not long after the 1850 Fugitive Slave Act took effect and a number of black leaders began to doubt the possibility of equality in the United States, Shadd emigrated to Canada. There she founded a school and, in 1853, helped to start a newspaper, the *Provincial Freeman*. The first black woman to edit a newspaper, Shadd raised funds for the paper by lecturing in Canada and the United States, urging American blacks to settle in Canada. Her staunch support of integration with whites put her in opposition with many black leaders in Canada, and her relations with them worsened when she claimed that the Refugee Home Society, a relief organization for black immigrants, was plagued with embezzlement and fraud.

Cary married in 1856 and, after her newspaper shut down, sent letters supporting abolition to U.S. newspapers. She returned home during the Civil War and recruited black soldiers. Continuing to teach and write after the war, she called for boycotts of businesses that discriminated against blacks. Later in her life, Cary became involved in the women's suffrage movement and was one of the first black American women to earn a law degree when she graduated from Howard University in 1883.

Born free in Virginia, **John Mercer Langston** (1829-1897) was orphaned as a small boy and raised in Ohio, first by friends of his white father and then by relatives of his black mother. Educated at Oberlin College, Langston was a respected scholar and helped to organize the Ohio State Anti-Slavery Society. In 1854, he became one of the nation's first black lawyers and, in 1855, he was the first American black elected to public office when he became the township clerk of Brownhelm, Ohio, where he was the only black citizen. During the Civil War, he recruited black troops for the Union army.

In the Reconstruction period, Langston argued that suffrage was the most important issue for freed blacks. As its president, Langston helped to make the National Equal Rights League—created by the national black convention in 1864—the first politically effective national black organization. Langston also worked for the

144

Delegates gather at the 1873 convention of the National Equal Rights League. Under Langston's leadership, the group had met with President Andrew Johnson and lobbied the Reconstruction Congress to protect the interests of freed blacks.

Freedmen's Bureau and organized southern black voters for the Republican Party, defending its Reconstruction policies to white and black audiences. In the 1870s, Langston campaigned for the Republican Party and for equal rights for all blacks, drafting the legislation that became the Supplementary Civil Rights Act of 1875. When Reconstruction ended, Langston promoted a black exodus out of the South, declaring that southern blacks had been returned to virtual slavery.

Throughout the decades following the war, Langston sought to improve educational opportunities for blacks. He briefly headed Howard University and also supported industrial colleges and the integration of public schools. He held government appointments to the District of Columbia Board of Health and as a diplomat to Haiti. After a court decided that he had been defrauded of his seat, he served the last three months of a term in the U.S. Congress.

Robert Brown Elliott (1842-1884) was a newspaper editor, lawyer, and member of the U.S. Congress from South Carolina (1871-1875), where the state's black

Robert Brown Elliott (standing at left), who virtually controlled the Republican Party in his home state of South Carolina, fiercely defended civil rights while serving in the U.S. House of Representatives.

majority meant that blacks temporarily had political power. An influential member of South Carolina's Republican Party during Reconstruction, Elliott was militant and uncompromising in his demands for equality for blacks. Before the end of Reconstruction finished his political career, he successfully fought against voting restrictions and for a bill that banned discrimination in public accommodations and transportation in South Carolina and worked for the Civil Rights Act of 1875.

Although she was born a slave, **Anna Julia Cooper** (1859?-1964) was freed by Lincoln's Emancipation Proclamation as a young girl and received an excellent education. After teaching for several years, she went to Oberlin College and eventually earned a master's degree in mathematics. She began teaching at the M Street High School in Washington, D.C., in 1887, and would later become the school's principal. In 1892, she published *A Voice from the South*, a book that attacked both racism and sexism.

Throughout the 1890s, Cooper was active in the black women's club movement, helping Mary Church Terrell and others organize the Colored Women's League. She also established black community centers and black branches of organizations such as the YWCA and Camp Fire Girls. After studying for a number of summers at the prestigious Sorbonne in France, Cooper, at the age of 65, became the fourth black American woman to earn a Ph.D degree. She spent her later years writing and heading a school in Washington, D.C., that taught basic skills to poor black people.

"The First Vote," as illustrated in Harper's Weekly. By the end of the nineteenth century, many southern states passed laws that favored white control and limited voting rights for blacks.

Bibliography

Allen, Richard. *The Life Experience and Gospel Labors of the Rt. Rev. Richard Allen.* New York: Abingdon Press, 1960.

Aptheker, Herbert. *American Negro Slave Revolts.* 1963. Reprint, New York: International Publishers, 1987.

———. *Nat Turner's Slave Rebellion.* New York: Humanities Press, 1966.

Bentley, Judith. *Harriet Tubman.* New York: Franklin Watts, 1990.

Bernard, Jaqueline. *Journey Toward Freedom: The Story of Sojourner Truth.* New York: Norton, 1967.

Berson, Robin Kadison. *Marching to a Different Drummer: Unrecognized Heroes of American History.* Westport, CT: Greenwood Press, 1994.

Bisson, Terry. *Nat Turner: Slave Revolt Leader.* New York: Chelsea House Publishers, 1988.

———. *Harriet Tubman.* New York: Chelsea House Publishers, 1990.

Bradford, Sarah. *Harriet Tubman: The Moses of Her People.* Gloucester, MA: Peter Smith, 1981.

Davis, Marianna W., ed. *Contributions of Black Women to America.* Vol 2. Columbia, SC: Kenday Press, 1962.

Douglass, Frederick. *The Life and Times of Frederick Douglass.* 1892. Reprint, New York: Bonanza Books, 1962.

———. *Narrative of the Life of Frederick Douglass*. In *The Classic Slave Narratives*, edited by Henry Louis Gates Jr., 243-331. New York: New American Library, 1987.

Genovese, Eugene D. *Roll, Jordan, Roll*. New York: Random House, 1976.

Gray, Thomas. *The Confessions of Nat Turner*. In *A Documentary History of the Negro People in the United States*. Vol. 1, edited by Herbert Aptheker, 119-125. New York: Citadel Press, 1990.

Heidish, Marcy. *A Woman Called Moses*. Boston: Houghton Mifflin, 1976.

Litwack, Leon and August Meier, eds. *Black Leaders of the Nineteenth Century*. Urbana and Chicago: University of Illinois Press, 1988.

Mabee, Carleton and Susan Mabee Newhouse. *Sojourner Truth: Slave, Prophet, Legend*. New York and London: New York University Press, 1993.

McFeely, William S. *Frederick Douglass*. New York and London: Norton, 1991.

Macht, Norman L. *Sojourner Truth: Crusader for Civil Rights*. New York: Chelsea House Publishers, 1992.

Ofari, Earl. *"Let Your Motto Be Resistance:" The Life and Thought of Henry Highland Garnet*. Boston: Beacon Press, 1972.

Ortiz, Victoria. *Sojourner Truth, a Self-Made Woman*. Philadelphia: Lippincott, 1974.

Potter, Joan and Constance Clayton. *African-American Firsts: Famous, Little-Known, and Unsung Triumphs of Blacks in America*. Elizabethtown, NY: Pinto Press, 1994.

Salley, Columbus. *The Black 100: A Ranking of the Most Influential African Americans, Past and Present.* New York: Citadel Press, 1992.

Schor, Joel. *Henry Highland Garnet: A Voice of Black Radicalism in the Nineteenth Century.* Westport, CT: Greenwood Press, 1977.

Sicherman, Barbara, et. al, eds. "Mary Church Terrell." *Notable American Women: The Modern Period.* Vol. 4. Cambridge, MA: Harvard University Press, 1980.

Smith, Jessie C. *Black Firsts: 2,000 Years of Extraordinary Achievement.* Detroit: Gale Research, 1994.

Sterling, Dorothy. *Black Foremothers.* Old Westbury, NY: Feminist Press, 1979. Revised 1988.

Tragle, Henry Irving. *The Southampton Slave Revolt of 1831.* Amherst: University of Massachusetts Press, 1971.

Washington, Booker T. *Up From Slavery.* 1901. Reprint, New York: Penguin Books, 1986.

———. *The Story of My Life and Work.* Westport, CT: Greenwood Press, 1909.

Wesley, Charles H. *Richard Allen: Apostle of Freedom.* Washington, DC: Associated Publishers, 1969.

Wheat, Ellen Harkins. *Jacob Lawrence: The* Frederick Douglass *and* Harriet Tubman *Series of 1938-40.* Hampton, VA: Hampton University Museum, 1991.

After years of struggle and a bloody Civil War,
nineteenth-century abolitionists saw the day when
laborers in the cotton fields were no longer slaves.

152

Index

"Call to Rebellion" speech (Garnet), 57-58, 64-65
Campbell, Tunis, 141
Carver, George Washington, 116, 117
Cary, Mary Ann Shadd, 143-144
Catt, Carrie Chapman, 135
Cherry (wife of Nat Turner), 47-48, 49, 51, 52, 54
Chew, Benjamin, 16
Church, Charles B., 126
Church, Louisa Ayers, 126
Church, Robert Reed, 126, 128
Church, Thomas, 126, 132
Civil Rights Act of 1875, 147
civil rights movement, 13, 125, 134
Civil War, 91, 126, 141, 144; beginning of, 38, 66, 86, 102; final years of, 39, 104, 108; Harriet Tubman's role in, 102-104; outcome of, 68, 87
Clay, Henry, 69
Collins, John A., 80, 81
colonies, American, 7-8, 16
Colored American, 63
Colored Woman in a White World, A, 135
Colored Women's League, 131, 147
Columbian Orator, The, 74
Confederate States of America, 7, 39, 67, 86, 103, 104
Confessions of Nat Turner, The, 44, 49-50, 53
Congress, U.S., 8, 10, 12, 41, 67, 85-86, 117, 146
Constitution, U.S., 7, 13, 80, 84, 87
Cooper, Anna Julia, 147
Coordinating Committee for the Enforcement of the District of Columbia Anti-Discrimination Laws, 137

cotton gin, 10, 11
Cotton States and International Exposition, 118
Covey, Edward, 74-75
Crummell, Alexander, 62, 141-142

Dallas Street Methodist Church, 74
Davidson, Olivia A. (wife of Booker T. Washington), 114, 115-116
David Walker's Appeal, 140
Davis, Nelson (husband of Harriet Tubman), 104-105
Delany, Martin, 66, 82, 85
Douglass, Annie, 80, 85
Douglass, Charles Remond, 80, 87
Douglass, Frederick, 13, 34, 38, 65, 66, 70, 102, 129; autobiographies of, 75, 81; death of, 89, 116; early years of, 72-75; education of, 73-74; escape of, from slavery, 78; federal appointments of, 88; newspapers of, 82-83, 86; as public speaker, 13, 71, 80, 81, 86; support of, for violent resistance, 13, 38, 85; as teacher, 74, 75-76; work of, for American Anti-Slavery Society, 80, 82; work of, for Freedmen's Bureau and Bank, 87, 88. *See also* Bailey, Frederick Augustus
Douglass, Frederick, Jr., 80
Douglass, Lewis Henry, 79-80, 87
Douglass, Rosetta, 79
Douglass' Monthly, 83, 86
Du Bois, W. E. B., 121-122, 123, 133
Dumont, John, 30-31

154

East Baltimore Mental Improvement Society, 77
Elliott, Robert Brown, 146-147
Emancipation Proclamation, 6, 7, 39, 86, 125, 126, 147
emigration, black: to Africa, 27, 66, 68, 69, 85, 140, 142; to Canada, 27, 143; to Haiti, 26-27, 68; to Jamaica, 66, 68
Episcopal Church, 23

Ferguson, Washington, 108
Fifteenth Amendment, 88
55th and 54th Massachusetts Regiments (black regiments), 86, 87
Folger, Ann, 33
Folger, Benjamin, 33
Fort Sumter, 86
Foster, Colonel Wilbur F., 112-113
Fourteenth Amendment, 88
Francis, Nathaniel, 52
Frederick Douglass's Paper, 83
Free African Society, 19-21, 22
Freedmen's Bank, 87, 88
Freedmen's Bureau, 39, 87, 141, 144-145
Freedmen's Hospital, 39
Freedmen's Village, 39
Freedom's Journal, 26, 140
Freeland, William, 75, 76
Fruitlands, 34
Fugitive Slave Act of 1850, 98-100, 101, 143
fugitive slave laws, 60, 61, 98-100, 101, 143

Gabriel (leader of slave revolt), 46-47, 93
Gage, Frances, 36-37
Garfield, James A., 129
Garnet, Eliza (Mary), 58, 60

Garnet, Elizabeth (Hennie), 59, 60
Garnet, George, 59, 60
Garnet, Henry Highland, 13, 140, 142; belief of, in violent resistance, 13, 56, 57, 64-66, 69, 81; "Call to Rebellion" speech of, 57-58, 64-65; death of, 69; early years of, 58-60; education of, 60, 61-63; as Presbyterian minister, 56, 63, 66, 67; support of, for black emigration, 66, 68; as U.S. diplomat to Liberia, 57, 68
Garrett, Thomas, 58, 100, 104
Garrison, William Lloyd, 34, 35, 63-64, 71, 72, 80, 81, 82, 84, 85
Garrisonians, 63-64, 80, 85
General Colored Association of Massachusetts, 140
George (father of Henry Highland Garnet), 58-59
Giddings, Doras, 20
Gilbert, Olive, 36
Giles v. Harris, 122-123
Giles v. Teasley, 122-123
Gray, Thomas, 53
Green, Beriah, 63
Griffiths, Julia, 85

Haiti, 26, 68, 88, 146; slave revolts in, 46, 93
Hampton Normal and Agricultural Institute, 110, 111, 112, 113, 114
Hardenbergh, Johannes, 30
Harmonia, 38
Harpers Ferry, 46, 55, 85, 102
Harper's Weekly, 6, 148
Harriet Tubman Home for Aged and Indigent Colored People, 105

125, 133, 134
National Association of Colored
Women (NACW), 131-132
National Equal Rights League,
144, 145
National Federation of Afro-
American Women, 105, 131
National Negro Convention,
57, 64, 66, 80
Nell, William, 82
New National Era, 83
newspapers: abolitionist, 37, 72,
80, 82, 140; black, 26, 63, 82,
83, 84, 86, 140, 143
New York Manumission
Society, 60
Niagara Movement, 133
Northampton Association, 34
North Star (guide on
Underground Railroad), 76,
94, 97, 100
North Star, 82, 83, 84
Noyes Academy, 62

Oberlin College, 128, 130, 144,
147
Ohio State Anti-Slavery
Society, 144
Old Bridget (grandmother of
Nat Turner), 43, 44
Oneida Theological Institute,
63

patrollers, 93, 96
peanut, 116, 117
Peter (son of Sojourner Truth),
30, 31
Philadelphia Vigilance
Committee, 98, 100, 143
Phillips, Wendell, 71
Phipps, Benjamin, 54
Pierson, Elijah, 31-32, 33
Pitts, Helen (wife of Frederick

Douglass), 88, 89
plantations, cotton, 10, 152
Presbyterian churches, 63, 66
Protestant Episcopal Church of
America, 23
Provincial Freeman, 143

Quakers, 10, 47, 58, 78, 93, 97

Reconstruction, 68, 88, 144,
145, 147
Reese, Giles, 48, 49, 51, 54
Refugee Home Society, 144
religion, importance of to
abolitionists, 12, 16, 17, 38,
140
Republican Party, 86, 88, 135,
145, 146-147
revolts, slave, 43, 44-47, 54, 64,
93; led by Nat Turner, 49-
53, 55
Revolution, American, 8, 11, 13,
17
Ricketson, Joseph, 79
Roosevelt, Theodore, 121, 122
Ross, Araminta (Minty), 92. *See
also* Tubman, Harriet Ross
Ross, Benjamin, 92, 95
Ross, Harriet Greene, 92, 96
Ruffner, General, 109
Ruffner, Viola, 109-110
Ruggles, David, 34, 78, 79

St. George's Methodist Church,
15, 19, 20, 21-22, 24
St. Thomas Episcopal Church,
23
Santo Domingo, 46
*Scenes in the Life of Harriet
Tubman*, 105
Scott, Dred, 12
segregation, 21, 108, 118, 120,

157

ABOUT THE AUTHOR

KIMBERLY HAYES TAYLOR, a native of Louisville, Kentucky, is a reporter for the *Star Tribune* newspaper in Minneapolis. She writes about issues that concern young people, the poor, and people of color. Taylor, who graduated from Morehead State University in 1984, has written for the Louisville *Courier-Journal*, the *Hartford Courant*, and *USA Today*. She is also the author of *Black Civil Rights Champions*.

Photo Credits